THE ECONOMICS OF
APARTHEID

THE ECONOMICS OF APARTHEID

Stephen R. Lewis, Jr.

Council on Foreign Relations Press

New York • London

COUNCIL ON FOREIGN RELATIONS BOOKS

The Council on Foreign Relations, Inc., is a nonprofit and non-partisan organization devoted to promoting improved understanding of international affairs through the free exchange of ideas. The Council does not take any position on questions of foreign policy and has no affiliation with, and receives no funding from, the United States government.

From time to time, books and monographs written by members of the Council's research staff or visiting fellows, or commissioned by the Council, or written by an independent author with critical review contributed by a Council study or working group are published with the designation "Council on Foreign Relations Book." Any book or monograph bearing that designation is, in the judgement of the Committee on Studies of the Council's board of directors, a responsible treatment of a significant international topic worthy of presentation to the public. All statements of fact and expressions of opinion contained in Council books are, however, the sole responsibility of the author.

Library of Congress Cataloguing-in-Publication Data

Lewis, Stephen R.
    The economics of apartheid / by Stephen R. Lewis, Jr.
      p. cm.
    Bibliography: p.
    Includes Index.
    ISBN 0-87609-056-0 : $17.95
    1. South Africa—Economic conditions. 2. South Africa—
      Economic policy. 3. Apartheid—Economic aspects—
      South Africa—History.
I. Title.
HC905.L49 1989
330.968'063–dc20
                                    89–1451
                                     CIP

90 91 92 93 94 95 PB 10 9 8 7 6 5 4 3 2 1

CONTENTS

v

LIST OF FIGURES AND TABLES

FIGURES

TABLES

For my parents

Stephen Richmond Lewis
Esther Magan Lewis

who always taught us that
color, class, or creed had
no role in determining a person's worth

This project was made possible by a generous grant from The Ford Foundation to the Council on Foreign Relations. Responsibility for seeing this book through to publication was shared by Michael Clough and Suzanne Hooper. For their assistance with this project the Council would also like to thank Michelle Bassin, Nomsa Daniels, John de St. Jorre, William H. Gleysteen Jr., Sue Roach, and Olivia Snaije.

PREFACE

I first began studying South Africa seriously when I went to work in Botswana in 1975 as an economic consultant to the Ministry of Finance and Development Planning. Botswana's policymakers needed to know about developments in neighboring South Africa because of the Republic's position as the dominant economic power in the southern African region. It quickly became apparent to me that South Africa's economy was analyzed by those outside the country in a cursory fashion, and that economists in South Africa itself tended either to analyze issues in a macroeconomic framework as if apartheid did not exist or to focus almost exclusively on microeconomic issues, such as labor markets, poverty, and income distribution. Important as those approaches may be, the relationship between the apartheid system and patterns of economic growth, and the constraints this relationship imposes on policy options were, I thought, largely being ignored.

As interest in South Africa began to rise sharply in the United States in the mid-1980s, it became clear that few American economists know much about the economies of South Africa and the region. During 1985–1986, I was frequently invited to seminars and conferences and asked to give presentations on the South African economy, not, I think, because of any special expertise, but because I was practically the only game in town. During that year Paul Kreisberg and Jennifer Seymour Whitaker of the Council on Foreign Relations suggested that I undertake an analysis of the South African economy that might contribute to a clearer understanding of how it functions. This seemed potentially useful because so much discussion of public policy in the United States and Europe, as well as in the United Nations, the Commonwealth, and other bodies, focused on economic issues such as the effects of trade and financial sanctions against the South African government.

The Economics of Apartheid is not a prescriptive book. Rather, it was written to help provide an understanding of the problems of South Africa and the possible consequences of various alternative policies both in South Africa and in the international community. I hope that it will be useful to policymakers and to all those concerned with the struggle for human rights in South Africa. My own perspective on South Africa is made clear in the introduction.

I am grateful to four institutions for supporting the research and writing of this book. Most of the work was undertaken between April and August of 1987 while I was on a sabbatical leave from Williams College as a visiting fellow at the Institute for Development Studies at the University of Sussex. The institute was a most congenial place for research and writing, and I am grateful to its fellows, and particularly to its director, Mike Faber, for their hospitality and support. The Council on Foreign Relations provided financial support as well as a critical forum for several presentations of my work in progress. Carleton College, which I joined in September 1987, agreed to postpone my arrival there so that I could continue on this project.

One accumulates many debts in writing a book. I learned the most about the South African economy while I was working in Botswana between 1975 and 1987. My colleagues there—in the government and in the Bank of Botswana—provided both insight and criticism of my own analyses: Because of their official positions, I will not mention them by name. Participants at a number of seminars and lectures between 1985 and 1987 in the United States and in the United Kingdom also provided a critical audience. The Council on Foreign Relations organized two seminars to review the entire manuscript when it was in draft form, and these provided valuable input. Over the years I have benefited from numerous discussions on the subject with Michael Clough, Wayne Fredericks, Charles Harvey, David Hauck, Helen Kitchen, and Jennifer Whitaker. For their careful readings and constructive criticism, I particularly want to thank Coralee

Bryant, Michael Clough, Wayne Fredericks, Reginald Herbold Green, David Hauck, Jeffrey Herbst, Thomas Karis, John Knight, Steven Mufson, Linda Robinson, Roy Stacy, and Franklin Williams. A number of South Africans, living at home or abroad, black and white, in the public and private sectors, in universities, and of widely divergent political persuasions, also provided me with valuable commentary. I do not list them so that my views cannot in any way be attributed to them, or vice versa, but I thank them individually and collectively for their thoughtful examination of my analyses. Their interest in searching for workable solutions to their country's enormous problems must give one some hope for the future.

Between April and September 1987, Julia Cross at the institute in Sussex served as my research assistant, secretary, and manager, balancing my six separate research projects, including this one, which were running simultaneously and were using four different style requirements, two different word processing systems, and both American and English spelling. She managed it all, including the production of the complete review draft of this manuscript, with great efficiency and good cheer, and she has my heartfelt thanks and admiration.

Families bear the costs of writing projects. Mine is no exception, and I thank them for putting up with yet more absences of both body and mind. Because of our extensive time living in southern Africa, my wife Gayle and our three children share my interest in the region, and in its people and their problems. Gayle read the manuscript, some chapters more than once, and her critical comments are happily incorporated into the final product. Virginia, Deborah, and Mark encouraged—and nagged—me to complete the project.

This book is dedicated to my parents, Stephen Richmond Lewis and Esther Magan Lewis. They shared a bit of Africa with us some years ago. But I particularly thank them here for their lessons, both of precept and of example, on the importance of tolerance and on the senselessness and immorality of prejudice on matters of race and religion.

Stephen R. Lewis, Jr.

Northfield, Minnesota
December 1989

INTRODUCTION

Apartheid, South Africa's unique system of legally prescribed racial segregation and white domination, has made the country a major focus of international attention since 1960. Although apartheid is fundamentally a political issue, economic arguments have always been central to the debate over "what to do about South Africa." However, the relationship between economics and apartheid is a subject of considerable controversy, usually generating more heat than light. The purpose of this book is to examine the economic realities of South Africa—historical, contemporary, and prospective.

The relationship of economics to apartheid engenders several important debates. One concerns the connection between economic development and the apartheid system. At one extreme are those who argue that economic growth, by creating an increasingly integrated economy and workplace and a growing demand for skilled labor, will generate inexorable pressures on apartheid institutions, leading to improvements in both the economic and the political position of black South Africans.[1] At the other extreme are those who say that a century of economic development, particularly the four decades since World War II, has seen no improvement in the relative position of black South Africans. Indeed, the decades of the 1950s and 1960s, during which South Africa experienced exceptionally rapid economic growth, were precisely the years when political repression was the greatest and the basic institutions of apartheid became most highly developed.

Another important debate concerns the relationship of capitalism to apartheid. One view is that they are mutually reinforcing: apartheid serves the interest of capitalist classes by keeping

1

wages low and profits high, and for that reason capitalists support the government and its institutions. A direct assault on the institutions of capitalism is an essential element in the efforts to remove apartheid. A contrary view accepts the fact that capitalists benefited from a cheap labor policy in the early years of the mining industry. But the institutions of apartheid, which prohibit the free movement of labor, prevent the education and training of workers—thus causing skill shortages—and impose unnecessary political, administrative, and social burdens, have made most large-scale capitalists opponents of apartheid.[2]

A third issue is the role of foreign investors in South Africa. By accelerating development, increased foreign investment may either reinforce or help break down apartheid, depending on one's viewpoint. Some argue that foreign companies have been a bulwark of the apartheid system, benefiting from cheap labor, supporting the government's policies, and bringing in necessary technology and products, often in contravention of internationally agreed boycotts. Another position, maintained with equal vigor, is that at least since the late 1970s foreign companies have been at the forefront of the movement for change in the apartheid system, making major reforms in employment practices and training programs that have influenced the policies and practices of South African companies.

The nature of South Africa's economy is also a subject of considerable debate. In one view it is a highly vulnerable, open economy, sensitive to international pressure through trade or investment boycotts. Such measures can therefore be used to change the basic approach of the South African government, since Pretoria will want to avoid paying serious economic costs. An alternative view is that the economy is robust, diversified, and capable of withstanding considerable external pressure and deprivation for a long time.

Related to international economic pressures is the debate about South Africa's role as the leading supplier of strategic minerals outside the Soviet bloc. Some analysts suggest that South Africa's supplies are vital to the West and that any actions disrupting their availability could involve substantial costs to Western interests. Others, pointing to the small total value of

South Africa's foreign trade and to the possibilities for substitution and recycling of metals, conclude that disruptions of South African supplies would cause little more than momentary inconvenience.

Finally, observers have different views on the changes that have occurred in South Africa during the past ten to fifteen years. Some argue that reforms in education, the legalization of black trade unions, changes in wage policies and wage levels, reductions in both legal and customary job discrimination, expansion in spending for social services, and the abolition of formal influx control represent fundamental shifts in the nature of the South African political and economic system. Others hold that these changes are a mixture of mild palliatives and measures aimed at creating and co-opting a black middle class. They argue that they have had no significant impact on the position of the majority of South Africans or on the nature of the system.

What is the evidence? What constitutes a balanced assessment of the facts? The protagonists in these debates have a tendency to claim that the glass is either bone dry or brim full. Is there a way of establishing where we are? And what might be the consequences of future internal developments in South Africa and external actions toward that country?

This book is written with a conviction that economic analysis can provide some insight into the problems facing South Africa. Since so much of the discussion about the country centers on economics, it seems worth trying to examine the issues in a relatively dispassionate way, using the approach of a rather conventional economist.

Over 50 years ago, Alfred Hoernle, a prominent white opponent of racial discrimination, delivered an address on segregation to the annual meeting of the South African Institute of Race Relations.[3] Two kinds of segregation existed, he said: "single-minded" segregation and "double-minded" segregation. The first was based on relegating native labor to the reserves, from where it migrated temporarily to the white areas, but under conditions of territorial, social, economic, and political segregation. This would not work, Hoernle asserted, because the whites were too dependent on native labor. Moreover, the "break-up of

Native society and culture" and the "proven vitality and adaptability of the Native peoples" meant that "political, economic, and social subjection is bound in the end to fail." The second, double-minded segregation, seemed to be more plausible, since it involved not just a privileged position for whites but "development of the Native group," which would necessitate, among other things, an enlargement of the native reserves. Nevertheless, Hoernle argued, this strategy was also flawed. "A civilized group, such as the Natives, under this policy ultimately . . . will not consent to permanent political inferiority." Double-minded segregation would eventually lead to a choice of: (a) reverting to single-minded segregation, (b) admitting the native group to share in political power, or (c) making segregation complete, by the establishment of economically and politically self-contained native states. Hoernle ended his speech with the hope that "our choice be guided by more wisdom than has been apparent so far."

Hoernle's wish has not been fulfilled. Moreover, his argument that the objectives of racial segregation and white domination are irreconcilable with a prosperous economy has been consistently ignored. The South African government has made various attempts to avoid integrating the majority population. Initially, there was a move toward single-minded segregation, and later came the development of completely self-contained units. Both strategies failed because neither made economic sense—even if they could have been politically implemented. In much of what follows, the tension between the forces leading toward greater integration of society—which seems inherent in modern economic growth—and South Africa's legal framework—developed in order to maintain white superiority and segregation—plays a central role.

It is important to set out my own position on the fundamentals of South Africa's political future. The Commonwealth Eminent Persons Group (EPG) on Southern Africa phrased the matter well, saying it wished to encourage "a genuine approach to power-sharing: an approach which accepted the ending of apartheid and sought a negotiated settlement under which a non-racial and truly representative government would be established and the legitimate rights of minorities protected."[4] Like the EPG, I offer no constitutional blueprint, but note that some form of universal franchise must be part of any solution that would be acceptable to the majority of South Africans, and that some form of protection for minorities, without veto power for any minority group, seems essential as well.

The EPG also noted that "the various reforms undertaken or foreshadowed to date must be viewed against the background of a determination not to give up white control."[5] My own reading of the so-called reforms that have taken place since the 1970s is consistent with this interpretation. It is hardly surprising, therefore, that the majority of South Africans do not regard the reforms as indicating fundamental changes in the system.

While the level of violence in South Africa has varied from year to year, the trend over the past three or four decades is clear. A failure to move toward a nonracial representative government and a commitment to give up the white monopoly of power can only increase the scale of violence. White domination will end; the questions are how and when. It is my hope that a clearer understanding of the economic realities in South Africa will assist both South Africans, who must be the prime movers, and outsiders in the search for fresh options and lasting solutions.

1

THE ORIGINS OF THE APARTHEID ECONOMY

The building blocks of the South African economy were laid over the three centuries between the first visit of the Dutch East India company's ships, under the command of Jan Van Riebeck, in 1652, and the election victory of the National Party in 1948. South Africa had already been inhabited, albeit sparsely, for millennia by the indigenous San and Khoikhoi, or Bushmen and Hottentots, as the Europeans called them. Sometime before the year 300, Bantu-speaking Africans entered the country from the north, fanning out slowly with their herds of cattle in a southerly and easterly direction. Following Van Riebeck's visit, the Dutch began to settle in and around Cape Town. They were joined by French Huguenots in 1689 and later by German immigrants. Gradually pushing inland, these European settlers blended to form a distinctive group of people who began calling themselves Afrikaners. Turning their backs on Europe, the Afrikaners developed their own language (Afrikaans), followed a fundamentalist strain of Calvinism, and lived for the most part as farmers. During Dutch rule, which lasted until 1795, when the British took over, slaves were imported from other parts of Africa and from East Asia, adding new elements to the racial and cultural mixture of people.

The British conquest of the settled area at the tip of South Africa led to an influx of British settlers, greater governmental control, and a more liberal set of laws and practices. Britain's emancipation of the slaves in 1834 was the last straw for many Afrikaners, or Boers (farmers), as they had come to be known. Several thousand of them, with their ox wagons, cattle, families, and servants, headed north into what became the Orange Free State and the Transvaal, and finally east over the Drakensberg Mountains into Natal. The territory they moved into was not empty. Much of it was inhabited by African pastoralists who contested the Afrikaners' advance. The critical battle was against the Zulus, under King Dingaan, at Blood River in 1838. A few hundred Afrikaners formed a laager of ox wagons and with their rifles held off vastly superior numbers without loss, killing some 3,000 Zulus who had no firearms. The Great Trek and the Battle of Blood River hold a revered place in the history and mythology of the Afrikaners. The practical result was the establishment of white settler superiority in much of the region, leading to the foundation of two Afrikaner republics. The British annexed part of Natal to prevent Afrikaner control of the Indian Ocean ports, and recognized Afrikaner independence in the Transvaal in 1852 and in the Orange Free State in 1854. They also brought in thousands of indentured laborers from India to work in Natal's sugar plantations. Most of the Indians stayed when their contracts expired, forming yet another distinct group in South Africa's complex society.

DIAMONDS AND GOLD

The economic shape of modern South Africa began to take form with the discovery of diamonds at Kimberley in 1867 and gold in the Transvaal in 1887. By the early 1880s diamonds made up 40 percent of the country's exports, and by the turn of the century gold and diamonds accounted for about 65 percent of total exports, which had more than quadrupled in the preceding 30 years. On the eve of World War I, mining represented 27 percent of gross domestic product (GDP) and South Africa was accounting for nearly 40 percent of the world's gold production. Diamonds and gold transformed the country from an agricultural and trading backwater to an economic resource of great value. They also set in motion the basic forces—economic, legal, demographic, and political—that have governed the development of modern South Africa ever since.

The discovery of diamonds and gold served as a magnet,

attracting foreign miners and investors seeking high profits. White immigrants came, largely from Europe, in numbers that quickly changed the population balance in the mining areas. An average of 24,000 immigrants arrived in South Africa annually between 1890 and 1913. By 1910 only 27 percent of white gold miners had been born in South Africa: the rest were immigrants, the vast majority from Britain.[1]

Blacks throughout southern Africa also migrated to the mines in search of work. The rapid growth in the number of blacks living and working in close proximity with whites aroused the latter's fears. As the gold mines expanded, the demand for labor began to outrun the flow of migrants. The gold mining companies realized that competition for black unskilled laborers could lead to wage increases. The result was the development in 1896 of a centrally organized labor recruiting system for black migrants from throughout southern Africa, who were housed in dormitories without their families; that system continues to the present day.

Foreign capital, principally British, flowed in to finance the new mining ventures—£145 million before World War I, or the equivalent of several billion dollars at today's prices—as South Africa's fabulous mineral wealth made a dramatic impact on the consciousness of European and North American investors. A few large companies, which provided finance, management, and technical skills for a number of individual mines, came to dominate the gold industry. Financial resources, control, and management of the mining houses were chiefly in the hands of English-speaking, and notably Jewish, South Africans, although most of the stock in these companies was owned by foreigners. The virtual exclusion of Afrikaners from the gold and diamond mining industries led to strong anti-British and anti-Semitic feelings. However, the Afrikaners retained their numerical superiority among South Africa's white population.

The new wealth, and the flow of English-speaking migrants, presented a number of problems to President Paul Kruger's Afrikaner republic in the Transvaal. Frequent conflicts arose over legal issues, over language, over life-styles. The Transvaal and its sister republic, the Orange Free State, were also threatened by Britain, which controlled the Cape and Natal, South Africa's other two provinces. The most immediate threat came from Cecil Rhodes, a man of vaulting ambition who had made a fortune in the Kimberley diamond mines and later became prime minister of the Cape Province. Rhodes's ultimate goal was to link Britain's African possessions by a railroad running through the continent from Cape Town to Cairo. Kruger, on the other hand, sought to develop a rail link between the Transvaal and the Indian Ocean in Portuguese-held Mozambique in order to make the burgeoning mining industry of his landlocked republic independent of the outlets controlled by Britain in the Cape and Natal provinces.

The tensions between Boer and Briton, which had been present from the earliest days of British settlement in the Cape, grew with the extension of British influence in the gold mining industry in the Transvaal. The outcome was the Anglo-Boer War (1899–1902), which the British won, but at an unexpectedly high cost. Britain's "scorched earth" policy, adopted to deprive the Boers' marauding commandos of their means of support, and the concentration camps in which some 25,000 Afrikaner women and children died had a traumatic impact on the Afrikaners. The bitter legacy of the war still conditions many Afrikaners' attitudes toward English-speaking South Africans in particular and toward outsiders in general.

In 1910 Britain created the Union of South Africa, bringing together its four provinces, and made it a self-governing "dominion" under the British crown. The country's new constitution, drafted by an all-white South African convention, limited parliamentary representation to whites. The right to vote, restricted to males, varied: whites only were eligible in the Free State and Transvaal; blacks not already registered could not do so in Natal; and franchise was based on literacy and property, not race, in the Cape. The constitution retained pieces of legislation from pre-Union days, such as the Masters and Servants acts, which entrenched rights for whites at the expense of blacks.[2] It also permitted South Africa to include three small neighboring territories—later to become Botswana, Lesotho, and Swaziland—in a Southern African Customs Union.

By 1910, therefore, a number of institutions, attitudes, laws, and practices were in place. Mining had become the mainstay of the economy, organized around mining finance houses with a large input of foreign capital; the migrant labor system for recruiting black mine workers throughout southern Africa was established; restrictions on both jobs and franchise by race had been imposed; the use of the trade and transport system for political and strategic purposes was a fact of life; and the conflicting interests of white and black, and of English- and Afrikaans-speaking whites, were clear.

South Africa's already highly regulated and segregated system was soon further strengthened. In 1911 the Native Labor Regulation Act made it a criminal offense for an African to break a labor contract. In the same year, the Mines and Works Act specified that certificates of competency for skilled jobs would not be granted to blacks in the Transvaal or the Orange Free State; certificates granted in Natal and the Cape would not be honored in the other provinces. The act also codified the ratios of white to black workers. In 1913 the Native Land Act created reserves of 91,000 square kilometers (about 7.5 percent of South Africa's total land area) in which no whites could purchase land without permission of the government, and threw up barriers to the purchase of freehold land by Africans in the rest of the country.

TWO WORLD WARS

While the economy had expanded greatly during World War I, the postwar period brought recession. Economic conditions had a major effect on the government's racial policies. In 1922 a major strike by white mine workers, the Rand Rebellion,[3] was triggered by the mining companies' decision to increase the ratio of black to white workers as a measure of cost control. The government adopted several measures to strengthen the position of whites vis-à-vis blacks, notably the Native Urban Areas Act, which required local authorities to set aside segregated areas for black residence and established machinery for influx control and the removal of "surplus" persons. But the incumbent government still lost the 1924 election.

The new "Pact" government, a coalition of the predominantly English-speaking Labor Party and the Afrikaner Nationalist Party, took a new tack. It tried to heal Afrikaner-English divisions and steer the society toward a structure drawn on class and racial lines. It sought to protect the economic interests of its Afrikaner and English supporters with legislation and administrative rulings. Its "civilized labor policy" involved paying whites at a higher rate than blacks for doing unskilled or semiskilled jobs. The policy was adopted in the civil service and complemented the color bar in the mines. While there was no legal color bar in manufacturing at that time, the policy was used as a basis for giving preference in government contracts and in requests for tariff protection. Beginning in 1925 the government changed the tariff structure and reorganized the Board of Trade and Industries, established four years earlier, to protect local industries in an effort to create jobs. The state-controlled Iron and Steel Corporation was founded in 1928 to further local industrial development. The 1924 Industrial Conciliation Act, which effectively excluded blacks, permitted the white unions to set the apprenticeship rules for training and to establish staffing ratios by race, thus giving them the power to shut out blacks.

The Great Depression brought a period of economic contraction in South Africa. However, the institutions established to protect the white working class through the civilized labor policy did their work. As total employment in manufacturing contracted between 1929 and 1933, white employment actually rose, and the loss of jobs was disproportionate among blacks. Moreover, the laws restricting the movement of blacks and their right to acquire land were strengthened in 1930 and 1937.

During the 1920s and 1930s considerable attention was focused on the problem of "poor whites" in South Africa—some 200,000–300,000 landless Afrikaners who had left low-productivity farming in rural areas but lacked the education and skills needed for modern-sector jobs. A number of factors virtually solved the problem. From 1933 the economy began to boom: the abandonment of the gold standard meant the local price of gold rose by 50 percent. The growth of protected industries; job creation in South African Railways and other state enterprises; and the civilized labor policy, which created nearly 100,000 jobs for whites between 1932 and 1939—all contributed.

At the same time, the government was giving some attention to the rural areas. The Native Reserves were expanded in 1936 to 12 percent of total land area. The Marketing Act of 1937 introduced state control into agricultural marketing, aimed not just at short-term stabilization of farm prices but also at maintaining farm incomes, including provisions for subsidizing export sales if surpluses could not be disposed of in domestic markets. Attention to the level of farm prices (affecting almost exclusively the marketed output from white farms), influx control designed to prevent blacks from moving to the urban areas, and restrictions on the availability of farm land to blacks all assured white farmers a sizable flow of low-wage black labor. Notwithstanding the government's support of the white farmers, the impact of industrial policy was greater. By the eve of World War II the contribution of manufacturing, construction, and public utilities to GDP was one and one-half times that of agriculture and three-quarters that of mining.

World War II brought some fundamental shifts in the economy. The manufacturing sectors expanded rapidly—employment grew by 50 percent in six years—in response to the wartime isolation of southern Africa from sources of supply in Europe. By 1945 GDP in industry, broadly defined, exceeded that of mining by nearly 50 percent and of agriculture by more than 60 percent. Absorption of whites into the armed forces led to a substantial increase in the ratio of black to white workers in manufacturing (from 1.5:1 in 1938–1939 to 2.2:1 in 1944–1945) and an increase in the number of skilled jobs held by blacks. South Africa came out of the war in a strong financial position, holding substantial foreign exchange reserves. A wave of new immigrants and a generally strong economy increased the country's appeal for foreign capital.

Thus on the eve of the 1948 election, the migrant labor system in mining had been established for half a century; influx control into urban areas and restrictions on blacks' trade union activity and ability to own land had been in place for several decades; the Native Reserves were long established and had been augmented in an effort to prevent excessive migration to the urban areas; the color bar had been operating in mining for over fifty years, and in manufacturing, government, and state-owned corporations for over twenty. In short, the basic instruments of separation were firmly in place.

However, the development of the economy and the substantial structural changes had not only brought the vast majority of whites into the modern sectors of the economy, but had also drawn nearly 2 million blacks into urban employment. Since virtually all the jobs were located outside the reserves, the integration of the black labor force with the white-owned economy was visible to all. Further, the greater skills acquired by black South Africans during World War II had raised their consciousness to an unprecedented level. The conflicts that Alfred Hoernle had described were developing rapidly, and a choice would have to be made to resolve them. That choice lay between single-minded segregation, power sharing, and comprehensive economic and political separation.

APARTHEID

The National Party, representing militant Afrikanerdom, unexpectedly won the election in 1948 and has remained in power ever since. Relying on the support of Afrikaner farmers and urban semiskilled workers, the Nationalists promised to make whites secure and prosperous by separating the races and maintaining power in Afrikaner hands. Modest wartime reforms of racial policy were to be abolished. The new government assured white farmers that they would continue to have access to low-cost black labor and that white workers in the towns would be protected from black competition. Since Afrikaner ownership in mining, finance, banking, and manufacturing was minimal, the government decided to expand its control over the economy and use its influence and patronage to direct resources to Afrikaner business. When the Nationalists took over in 1948, English-speaking whites had nearly twice the income per capita of Afrikaners, while even as late as 1960 English-speakers were three times as likely as Afrikaners to hold the top jobs in commerce and industry.

Legislation and Control

The Nationalists' program for reshaping the economy and the society was based on racial classification and separation in all aspects of life in South Africa. A flood of legislation followed their installation. The Population Registration Act (1950) required that each person's race be defined. The Prohibition of Mixed Marriages Act (1949) made marriages between whites and other racial groups illegal, while the Immorality Act (a 1950 amendment to an existing law) prohibited sexual intercourse between whites and other races. The Group Areas Act (1950) specified where each race could live. The Bantu Act (1952) also known as the Abolition of Passes and Consolidation of Documents Act, created the "reference" (or pass) book, a comprehensive identity document that Africans had to carry at all times. The Native Laws Amendment Act (1952) tightened influx control. The Bantu Education Act (1952) instituted state control of education for Africans and established a new curriculum designed to prepare Africans for a lower place in the economy and society. A battery of security legislation was installed to suppress opposition.

The final blocks in the separatist wall of development for Africans were the laws establishing self-government—and ultimately "independence"—of the areas that had first been designated as Native Reserves but were later called homelands. The Bantu Authorities Act (1951) established government-appointed authorities in the reserves and abolished the fifteen-year-old Natives' Representative Council. Africans would be divided on the basis of their ethnic origin. Tribal authorities would be given some authority, but under white control. The Promotion of Bantu Self-Government Act (1959) identified *every* African with a reserve. Legislation between 1956 and 1970 established the individual territorial authorities for eight—later increased to ten—homelands, or "national units." The Bantu

Homelands Citizenship Act (1970) and related legislation provided for separate citizenship for each African individual in the appropriate tribal area. Finally, the Transkei homeland was declared "independent" in 1976; the definition of a Transkei "citizen" was broad enough to include anyone who spoke a language used there, regardless of whether the individual had ever been to the Transkei. Bophuthatswana, Venda, and Ciskei also became "independent" during the next five years, rendering some nine million South Africans "foreigners" in their own country.

The homelands policy had important political and economic implications. Africans deemed to be citizens of independent homelands would exercise their political rights *there,* not in the rest of South Africa. On the economic side, a government commission reported in the 1950s that the homelands would require considerably more land to become economically viable. This finding was unacceptable to the Nationalist government, which adopted an alternative strategy that stressed the homeland origin and residence of migrant labor but allowed workers to become commuters or temporary residents in white South Africa. Black South Africans were to be regarded as "temporary sojourners," similar to the way that Turkish workers are viewed in West Germany. The government thereby hoped to retain the advantages of a black work force while making the homeland governments responsible for workers' social welfare. This is what Alfred Hoernle meant by single-minded segregation. Unfortunately for the government, much of the African labor force was not in the homelands when this strategy was devised. So, in order to implement it, the Nationalists uprooted millions of people from white areas during the next three decades and moved them to their respective "homelands," whether they had any real connection to those areas or not, and in most cases against their will.

Economic Change

For a considerable period the Nationalist strategy of single-minded segregation, or grand apartheid, as it was often called, seemed to produce excellent economic results for its white constituents. Fueled initially by the devaluation of the South African currency in 1949, which varied the local gold price substantially, and by an early inflow of foreign capital, the growth of real GDP was rapid by international standards, averaging over 5 percent annually from 1950 to 1970. The continued import substitution behind protective barriers, the development of the new gold fields in the Orange Free State, and other mining ventures provided a succession of profitable investment opportunities. The Afrikaners' economic position improved dramatically. Afrikaner business made major advances, and Afrikaners moved into positions of control in the state corporations. Subsidies continued for the agricultural sector, which was dominated by National Party supporters. Employment grew rapidly for all whites, whatever the level of education and skill, with everybody benefiting from the continued application of the color bar. And whites became increasingly urbanized. Even the shock of the Sharpeville massacre in 1960 was absorbed by the economy. Despite a flight of capital and negative net capital inflows from 1960 through 1964, the South African economy went from strength to strength.

Beneath the surface, however, several important economic forces were at work. The development of Bantu education and the use of the color bar in apprenticeship training were creating shortages of skills for the rapidly expanding economy. Administering and policing the apartheid system were absorbing increasing numbers of the available educated and skilled people, especially whites. The domestic market for mass consumption goods was not expanding as rapidly as it might have been because of the low and stagnant standards of living of the majority of the population. It became clear that the initial design of the homelands policy would not work. The migratory and commuter worker system was not generating the necessary jobs, and the government increasingly recognized that the homelands were not economically viable. Furthermore, pressures exerted by the international community pushed the government toward local production of goods whose supply was threatened by past or future embargoes.

Economic policy underwent significant modifications as the impossibility of implementing single-minded segregation, or grand apartheid, became increasingly clear. The main changes involved a growing recognition that economic activities had to be moved to the homelands, where a large proportion of the African population lived, that skill shortages engendered by racial restrictions were hamstringing economic growth, that the economy needed greater labor mobility, and that some Africans would have to be accepted as permanent residents in South Africa. The government's vision gradually shifted toward what Hoernle had described as double-minded segregation. This involved the development of separate political and administrative institutions and viable economic units for Africans, regardless of whether this made economic sense for the country as a whole.

After the mid-1970s it began to become evident that apartheid and the effort to maintain it was placing South Africa in an impossible economic and financial situation. The attempt to make the homelands more economically viable meant providing resources for homeland governments and incentives for businesses to locate there. A rising proportion of government expenditure, and national income, was devoted to this objective. But more than half a century of neglect could not be made up overnight, and progress was slow. The Arab oil boycott and other international pressures on South Africa increased the price South Africa paid for its crude oil; they also led to the development of an independent but very expensive source of liquid fuel in the shape of the SASOL coal gasification plants. Concern about trade embargoes convinced the government that it had to invest in import-substitution activities at relatively high capital costs and low levels of output. Domestic political unrest, combined with pressures from the Western industrialized countries, reduced the flow of capital into South Africa. The end of white rule in Angola, Mozambique, and Southern Rhodesia, which together had formed a protective buffer between South Africa and black Africa, brought increased expenditures for internal and external security and extended the geographic range of South Africa's economic, transport, and security concerns into the affairs of ten black-ruled countries in the region. The budget, and the budget deficit, grew as a percentage of national income.

Gold prices boomed in the late 1970s but did not check the slowdown in economic growth. Growth was flat in the 1980s, largely because of the increasing economic burden created by the government's commitment to apartheid. Growth could not absorb the expansion of the black labor force in the 1970s, and overt black unemployment rose rapidly in the 1980s. As the diseconomies inherent in apartheid became more obvious, major sections of the business community increasingly came to oppose government policy. They were motivated by growing recognition that sustained economic expansion would be impossible without changes in many of the basic features of apartheid, especially those that restricted the development of a stable, skilled black labor force. The cumulative economically disastrous effects of apartheid are summarized in chapter 6.

The dilemma facing the National Party government in the late 1980s is thus the same that Hoernle identified half a century ago. Should it return to its original vision of single-minded segregation, as the white parties to the right of the government advocate? Or should it "admit the Native group to power sharing," which the government says it wishes to do but has not yet made any serious effort to accomplish? Or should it establish politically and economically self-contained states, which is de facto government policy, but in South Africa's highly integrated economy simply will not work?

2

GROWTH AND STRUCTURE
OF SOUTH AFRICA'S ECONOMY

In studying the South African economy, it is helpful to trace the pattern of economic development and growth in other countries. The almost universal experience has been a change from an agricultural, subsistence, rural-based economy to one in which agriculture accounts for a very small share of output and employment, where manufacturing industry and related infrastructure constitute a very high share of output and employment, and where the vast majority of the population is urbanized. Numerous other changes take place as well. The share of national income saved and invested rises, the share of industrial goods in exports increases, and the public sector's contribution to total output grows. One of the fundamental mechanisms involved in the transformation of societies from low to high income is the growth of productivity of the labor force in all sectors of the economy.

The process of shifting labor from low-productivity subsistence agriculture into high-productivity activities in manufacturing and modern services (banking and finance, transportation, and so forth), as well as into higher-productivity agricultural activities, continues almost unabated as overall per capita income rises. It is a process that has been going on for two centuries. As opportunities arise for employment (or self-employment) in the expanding modern, high-income sectors, people move; as they move, income per head rises. Societies are initially dominated by a rural, largely subsistence economy of people with low levels of education and low productivity, and include a small urban industrial (or mining) high-income sector.

High-income countries are dominated by a large urban, industrial, high-income sector and have a relatively small subsistence sector, usually on small farms in rural areas; agricultural output in such countries is dominated by high-productivity farms, not necessarily large in scale. The process of transformation involves the growth of productivity in all sectors, combined with the shift of the population out of low-income agriculture.

Several points about this process of development are relevant to South Africa. First, in all countries the economy and the society will show evidence of "dualism." Some sectors—largely in agriculture, but in urban centers as well—are characterized by low productivity, family-centered organization for business and farming, substantial overt and disguised unemployment, often considerable landlessness in the agricultural sectors, and relatively low income per capita. In the modern sectors, by contrast, one finds larger organizations, wage employment at substantially higher skill and wage levels, more advanced technology, and correspondingly much higher income per capita. South Africa presents some extreme examples of this dualism, with important differences from the usual pattern.

Second, a phase of increasing inequalities of income often, though not universally, accompanies early stages of development. Not all people enter the modern sector simultaneously, and modern and "traditional" sectors typically show large differences in average incomes. Therefore, some individuals gain from the process before others do. Again, South Africa exhibits some of these characteristics, though with a distinctive racial bias. Because of discriminatory practices in education and access to skilled jobs, the white population has been drawn more rapidly into the high-income modern-sector jobs, while most of the black population has been relegated to the lower-paid unskilled and semiskilled positions.

Third, a critical element in the course of development is the increasing productivity of land and labor in agriculture. Indeed, one reason for increases in wages in the modern sectors is often the growth in productivity in agriculture in the traditional sectors: modern-sector wages must rise in order to attract people from the agricultural areas where incomes have gone up. This illustrates a key element in South Africa's situation. The land available to blacks has been severely restricted, and for a century government efforts—critical in virtually all cases of successful agricultural development—have been directed almost exclusively toward white farmers. As a result, the incomes available in the African and colored rural areas have remained pitifully low, leaving people no alternative to seeking work in the modern sectors, including white agriculture, at whatever wage is available. The subsistence sector as a provider of income for the majority of South Africans effectively ceased to exist decades ago: the population densities were simply too great to allow any but a fraction of the black population a genuine subsistence output; the rest have had to depend on wage labor in white areas of South Africa, both urban and rural.

The transformation of a country's economy and society involves the vast majority of its population, which in South Africa means blacks. It is inevitable that the development of the economy as a whole will draw increasing numbers of blacks into the modern, high-wage, high-productivity sectors. Extremes in segregation will ultimately present problems even in narrowly defined economic terms. Further, the demand for more highly skilled workers will exceed the numbers available from the minority white population, resulting in either a decrease in economic growth or changes in policy to allow blacks to gain skills and move up in the occupational hierarchy. The tension between simultaneously needing blacks' labor and wanting to exclude them from the white areas has been a theme in South African economic, social, and educational policies for decades.[1] Since the formation of the Union in 1910, South Africa's governments have never accepted the impossibility of reconciling these two desires.

South Africa has exhibited many features of a typical upper-middle-income developing country, especially one with rich mineral resources. At the same time, however, its pattern and rate of economic growth have been strongly influenced by apartheid. A brief survey of the growth and structure of South Africa's economy, examining the elements that make it typical as well as those that render it unique, will help clarify the problems that confront the country.

THE AGGREGATE RECORD

From 1911 through World War II, South Africa's population grew at a rate of about 2 percent per year (see Table 2.1). The growth rate accelerated after 1945, reaching an average of 3 percent annually during the 1970s. The rate of natural increase in recent years has been considerably higher for Africans than for whites. The white proportion of the total population appears to have peaked in 1921, remained relatively constant until just after the National Party was elected in 1948, and declined consistently ever since, dropping below 15 percent by 1985. By contrast, the share of the African population has increased from just over two-thirds at the time of the Union to nearly three-quarters today. This basic demographic shift has fundamental implications for the political and economic future of South Africa.

A key element of the demography is the importance of net immigration to the growth of the white population (see Appendix Table A). The vast majority of immigrants have been white. The South African government does not include black migrant workers from other countries in the region in its immigration and emigration statistics. These workers, who still account for half the total black work force in mining, are considered temporary residents. Over one million whites have immigrated since 1947, a significant proportion of the 1985 total white population of nearly five million. During the early years of National Party rule, net immigration was relatively low. Sizable net inflows began again in 1963, and lasted until 1976; during that period, net immigration averaged 30,000 per year. Net emigration followed the Soweto uprisings of 1976. The early 1980s saw substantial net immigration again, much of it coming from Zimbabwe. In the aftermath of the unrest that began with the adoption of South Africa's new constitution in 1984, there was again net emigration. In the early 1960s, when Kenya and Zambia became independent, and in the 1970s, as the war for independence in

TABLE 2.1. POPULATION OF SOUTH AFRICA AND PERCENT DISTRIBUTION OF POPULATION, BY RACE, 1911–1985

Year	African	Colored	Asian	White	Total	Growth rate (%)*
			Millions			
1911	4.02	0.52	0.15	1.28	5.97	—
1921	4.70	0.54	0.16	1.52	6.92	1.5
1936	6.60	0.77	0.22	2.00	9.59	2.2
1946	7.83	0.93	0.28	2.37	11.41	1.8
1951	8.56	1.10	0.37	2.64	12.67	2.1
1960	10.93	1.51	0.48	3.09	16.01	2.5
1970	15.34	2.05	0.63	3.77	21.79	2.7
1980	21.40	2.61	0.82	4.53	29.36	3.0
1985	24.57	2.86	0.90	4.83	33.16	2.5
			Percentage distribution			
1911	67.2	8.8	2.6	21.4	100	
1921	67.8	7.9	2.4	22.0	100	
1936	68.8	8.0	2.3	20.9	100	
1946	68.6	8.1	2.5	20.8	100	
1951	67.6	8.7	2.9	20.9	100	
1960	68.3	9.4	3.0	19.3	100	
1970	70.3	9.4	2.9	17.4	100	
1980	72.9	8.9	2.8	15.4	100	
1985	74.1	8.6	2.7	14.6	100	

Sources: For 1911–1970, D. Hobart Houghton, *The South African Economy,* 4th ed. (Cape Town: Oxford University Press, 1976), 170. For 1980 and 1985, author's estimates of numbers growth, based on C. Cooper et al., *Race Relations 1985* (Johannesburg: South African Institute of Race Relations, 1986). South African government sources no longer report figures for the country as a whole; these sources exclude the homelands that have been declared "independent."

* Annual compound growth rate since last date shown.

Zimbabwe intensified, a major portion of immigrants to South Africa was composed of people leaving countries that had achieved, or were close to achieving, majority rule.[2]

Table 2.2 shows the average annual growth rate of real GDP for various periods from 1919 to 1985. South Africa's rate of real economic growth generally averaged well over 5 percent annually for the half-century from the end of World War I through 1970. This was a very respectable record in international terms. However, the rate has consistently declined in every five-year period since 1970.

TABLE 2.2.   ANNUALIZED RATES OF GROWTH OF REAL GDP
AT FACTOR COST

Period	Growth rate (%)
1919–1929	5.0
1929–1939	5.8
1939–1949	5.8
1950–1960	4.4
1960–1965	6.0
1965–1970	5.4
1970–1975	4.0
1975–1980	2.8
1980–1985	1.1

Sources: For 1919–1949, D. Hobart Houghton, The South African Economy, 4th ed. (Cape Town: Oxford University Press, 1976), 40. For 1950–1985, South African Reserve Bank, Quarterly Bulletin, various issues.

From the time of the Union in 1910, South Africa has experienced the shifts in the structure of output and, to a large extent, the location of population that one would expect in a country with increasing income per capita. Data for 1911 and later are shown in Table 2.3. Agriculture has declined as a share of GDP and presently accounts for only about 5 percent, which is low by the standards of upper-middle-income economies. Mining has also decreased over time, from a dominant position of 27 percent of GDP just prior to World War I to 16 percent in 1985. It reached a low of 10 percent just prior to the freeing of the international gold price in 1971, and peaked at 22 percent in 1980 as gold prices rose to record heights. The importance of mining is above average for South Africa's per capita income and places the country in the same range as oil-producing states with larger populations, such as Algeria. The share of the industrial sector—broadly defined by the World Bank to include mining, manufacturing, construction, and public utilities (water, gas, and electricity)—is greater in South Africa than in other countries of similar income levels, primarily because of the large mining sector. This industrial sector has risen as a share of national income over time, though the dominant contributor has shifted from mining to manufacturing. Manufacturing itself has fluctuated between 20 percent and 25 percent of GDP in recent years, having benefited since the 1920s from the government's policies of protection and import substitution.

TABLE 2.3. PERCENTAGE DISTRIBUTION OF GDP BY SECTOR,
1911–1985

Year	Agriculture*	Mining	Industry†	All other	Total
1911–1912	17.4	27.1	6.7	48.8	100
1924–1925	19.9	17.4	12.4	50.3	100
1932–1933	12.2	24.3	13.6	49.9	100
1938–1939	12.6	20.7	17.7	49.0	100
1946	13.0	11.9	21.3	53.9	100
1950	17.8	13.3	22.9	46.0	100
1960	12.3	13.7	26.0	47.9	100
1970	8.1	10.0	30.0	51.8	100
1980	7.0	22.0	28.7	42.4	100
1985	5.2	16.1	29.5	49.1	100

Sources: For 1911–1939, D. Hobart Houghton, *The South African Economy*, 4th ed. (Cape Town: Oxford University Press, 1976), 42. For 1946–1985, South African Reserve Bank, *Quarterly Bulletin*, various issues.

* Includes fishing and forestry.
† Manufacturing, construction, electricity, water, and gas.

The shift in the origin of GDP has been matched by a somewhat similar shift in both the rural-urban distribution of the population and the structure of employment. The changes that have occurred in South Africa, despite the many restrictions imposed on the movement of the black population, are similar to those that have taken place in comparable countries since the end of World War II. The share of population considered urban rose from about 25 percent before World War II to nearly 40 percent at the end of the war, and has increased to something over 50 percent today. World Bank figures for upper-middle-income countries suggest that the ratio of urban to rural population in South Africa is relatively low. The reason is twofold. First, a relatively large segment of the black population is still rural. Second, many black workers illegally present in urban areas, and in some homeland areas, are classified as rural when, in reality, they reside in suburbs of major cities. The trend of rising urbanization is largely related to the growth of mining and manufacturing and to supporting infrastructure and services.

Among the key macroeconomic elements in development are a country's ability to invest a sufficient amount to generate added output and its ability to save enough from current income to finance such investment. South Africa has managed to sustain high levels of investment—between 25 percent and 30 percent of

GDP—in almost every year since World War II and thus lies comfortably in a category of countries that should be achieving rapid growth. The ability of South Africa to save and finance its investment is also high; gross domestic saving rose from 17 percent of GDP between 1946 and 1956 to a peak of 31 percent between 1977 and 1981, and remained at nearly 25 percent of GDP during the recession years 1982–1986. The ratios of gross domestic saving and investment to GDP are shown in Figure 2.1. (See also Appendix Table B.) The difference between domestic investment formation and domestic saving is met by capital inflow; if domestic saving is greater, it can finance an outflow of capital. The latter has been the case in recent years as South Africa has been repaying foreign debts and experiencing disinvestment by foreign companies. The key point is that South African saving rose in the postwar period at such a rate that it could finance investment of about 25 percent of GDP on a consistent basis without capital from abroad.

Finally, there is the issue of the inequality of the distribution of income. Data are generally hard to come by and are seldom available on comparable definitions through time or between countries. South Africa has collected considerable information on wage levels by race over time and by type of economic activity because of its history of racial separation. But less evidence is available on the "size distribution" of income—that is, the share of income received by households at various income levels. The data on racial distribution of income suggest that South Africa is among the most unequal of the upper-middle-income developing countries. Studies examining the distribution by level of household income indicate that it may also be more unequal in this respect. International comparative studies by Hollis Chenery and his associates suggest that countries specializing in the export of primary products, particularly minerals, are likely to have more unequal distributions of income.[3] Therefore, even in income distribution, the South African economy might not fall outside the "normal" range.

Thus, since the discovery of diamonds and gold over 100 years ago, South Africa's development has, in many important respects, followed the pattern associated with other upper-mid-

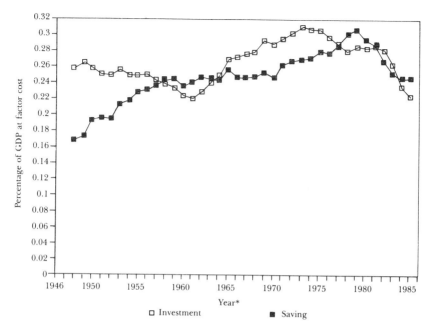

Source: South African Reserve Bank, *Quarterly Bulletin,* various issues.

*Figures are five-year averages, centered on the middle year.

FIG. 2.1. GROSS DOMESTIC SAVING AND INVESTMENT AS PERCENTAGE
OF GDP, 1947–1985*

dle-income, mineral-rich countries. Cities have grown, people have migrated and changed occupations, the economy has become more complex and interdependent, the share of income saved has risen, agriculture has declined, and industry has grown in relative importance. But South Africa parts company with other countries in that many of its economic problems are closely related to the fact that, while it was undergoing the processes of "normal" development, successive governments, particularly since World War II, attempted to frustrate the very interplay of economic forces that are a necessary part of sustained economic growth.

The 1980s have been a bad decade for the South African economy. Aggregate economic performance has been dismal. Between 1981 and 1987 real GDP rose a total of only 4.7 percent, and nonagricultural employment remained virtually stagnant; with population growing by almost 2.5 percent annually, per capita income declined by over 10 percent. In 1988 GDP finally increased at a rate slightly faster than population. Unemployment among whites, coloreds, and Asians quintupled. Among Africans residing outside South Africa's four "independent" homelands officially estimated unemployment had reached over one million people—some 18 percent of the economically active African population—by the third quarter of 1986. These figures understate the extent of the problem. From 1981 to 1987, annual investment in fixed assets dropped by 30 percent, and the quantity of imports fell by 27 percent. The value of the rand declined from $1.14 in 1981 to $0.40 in early 1989, at one time reaching $0.34. International capital flows turned from an inflow of $3.5 billion to an outflow of $3.7 billion between 1981 and 1986, and they remained negative in 1987 and 1988.[4] In 1985 South Africa's authorities were forced to declare a "standstill" on principal repayments of most of the country's external debt.

Even without the internal political problems created by apartheid, government and business leaders, who are all white, would have reason to worry about the economy in the late 1980s. For some time, significant sections of the business community have been at odds with the government over how to address the country's main economic, political, and social problems. The international community took a series of actions in the 1980s that have reduced South Africa's access to markets for exports, for imports of both goods and technology, and for investment capital. These actions potentially have major implications for South Africa's relatively open economy.

From the perspective of the majority of the population, rather than that of the government and business leadership, the state of the economy in the late 1980s is even worse. Most Africans—over 40 percent of all South Africans—live in the 13 percent of the country that comprises the homelands. Per capita production in the homelands amounts to less than 5 percent of the level in the rest of South Africa.[5] Because very few productive assets exist in these areas, residents depend either on long-term migration or on daily or weekly commuting to jobs in white areas of the country. A major part of the burden of downward adjustment in the economy after 1981 was borne by those black citizens who, in better times, might have found a job. Official figures suggest that by 1988 Africans were absorbing at least 95 percent of total unemployment, though they represent under 75 percent of the population. January 1988 figures showed 61,000 whites, coloreds, and Asians registered as unemployed, while sample surveys showed 924,000 unemployed Africans. However, the official figures exclude the four "independent" homelands, where roughly one-quarter of the African population resides. Their inclusion would raise the number of unemployed blacks to at least 1.5 million. Death rates, including infant and child mortality rates, remain higher for Africans than for other racial groups; Africans' access to education, health care, and other social services is significantly lower.

SOUTH AFRICA'S SPECIAL CIRCUMSTANCES

Before turning to the issue of racial segregation and discrimination, it is important to understand the effect of South Africa's rich mineral deposits on its historical development and present circumstances. First diamonds and then gold, and to a much lesser extent other minerals, have provided South Africa with an asset base of extraordinary value. Mining, particularly gold mining, is highly capital-intensive relative to output and requires large investments, which, in turn, usually need substantial gestation periods before producing returns. However, both gold and diamond mines have had low ratios of operating costs to total sales revenue for much of the past century. As a result, once the mines are operational, a large share of gross export sales goes either to the government revenue or to post-tax profits.

As he laid one of the first diamonds from Kimberley before the House of Assembly in the Cape, the secretary of state for the colonies said, "Gentlemen, this is the rock on which the future success of South Africa will be built."[6] Diamonds provided much of the initial capital for the gold mining industry in the Transvaal. Diamonds and gold together supported the development of rail transportation to the interior, provided direct government revenue, and effectively subsidized the import substitution, behind protectionist walls, that has led South Africa's industrialization for the past 60 years. Reinvested profits from gold and diamond mining have built much of the domestic industrial base in South Africa, a fact reflected by the dominance of the Anglo-American DeBeers group in the industrial and financial sectors of the economy. Over a century after the discovery of gold and diamonds, and despite enormous changes in the structure of production, these two sources still provide 40–50 percent of South Africa's visible export earnings. For every $10 the price of gold increases, South Africa's export earnings from gold rise by around $200 million per year. Whenever world markets become nervous about paper currencies or international political conditions, a rising gold price ensures a pure windfall transfer from the rest of the world to South Africa, and a major share to the government in tax revenue.

Discrimination in Access

The importance—and the fascination—of South Africa's gold and diamonds is undeniable. But the racial aspects of that country are the main features of its economic development and current stagnation. The racial dimension has been dominant throughout South Africa's modern economic growth. The consequences first of segregation and then of apartheid are evident both in the structure of South Africa's development and in the distribution of wealth.

For over a century, there has been systematic, legally enforced, differential access in South Africa to *all* the processes—acquisition of skills, migration to higher-paying jobs, ownership of land and reproducible assets, access to credit—by which individuals participate in economic development. This differential access, enforced most comprehensively since World War II, has had the greatest adverse effect on Africans but has also affected colored and Asian people.

Access to land for Africans was limited through the Native Land Act of 1913 and subsequent legislation. Asians had always been prohibited from residing in the Orange Free State, and their land rights in the Transvaal were restricted from 1885 onward. The Group Areas Act made it illegal for all persons of color to reside in the white areas of South Africa without government permission, and licenses to do business in an area by a "disqualified" person required government approval for renewal. African, Asian, and colored South Africans have been physically removed from white areas throughout the past four decades, generally losing much or all of the value of their accumulated assets, such as land and immovable structures. As no new freehold land tenure was allowed and little land was available under the permitted 30-year leasehold for Africans outside the homelands (extended to 99 years in recent reforms), an African had no way to purchase real property for investment purposes or even for home ownership. Tenure in the homelands was mainly on a communal basis. Land allocated to Africans constitutes only 13 percent of the total land area of South Africa. This land contains only a fraction of the country's mineral resources, principally platinum in Bophuthatswana. As a consequence of the various regulations on the ownership of land and natural resources, as well as licenses to trade and undertake business, the access of all South Africans of color, and particularly those destined for homeland citizenship, has been exceptionally restricted.

Access to jobs in the modern sectors has also been highly regulated by numerous customs, laws, and administrative practices. These have included the manning ratios of the late 1800s, specifying minimum numbers of whites per blacks in the mining industry; the civilized labor policy, beginning in the 1920s; and various legislative and administrative mechanisms dealing with job reservation. Whites have been given preferential access to all jobs, including unskilled jobs during a slump in general business conditions, as in the 1930s.[7] Furthermore, wage rates were higher for whites than for blacks holding the same job, even in the case of unskilled jobs. Thus, one mechanism for participating in general economic development—absorption into a growing modern sector—was severely restricted for blacks. Only since the mid-1970s, under the pressures of shortages of white labor for businesses of all sizes, and increasing social and political pressure on large businesses, has this basic discrimination against black unskilled labor begun to break down.

During the periods of rapid economic expansion in the 1950s, the 1960s, and the early 1970s, the growing shortage of skilled white workers led to an increasing erosion of the color bar and a less strict observance of job reservation. Official efforts to deal with labor shortages began in the early 1970s, even before the labor unrest, and included raised ceilings for expenditure on Bantu education and expansion of the range of skilled jobs for which blacks could qualify. The process accelerated in the 1970s. Labor reforms recommended by the Wiehahn Commission in 1979 had removed most legal job reservation by 1984, though the white-only Mine Workers Union still vociferously opposed issuing blasting certificates to blacks. Custom in the workplace continued to provide effective job reservation in many establishments. But since the mid-1970s the removal of legal restrictions, combined with intensified international pressures on many companies, has eased access to promotion in many sectors of the economy, particularly among larger and foreign-owned firms in the private sector. Perhaps more than half of the narrowing in black-white wage differentials over the past decade can be attributed to blacks' increased access to jobs associated with higher skills and incomes.[8]

Major problems remain for blacks despite an erosion of some aspects of job reservation. Perhaps the most serious is that of education and training. One element, the continued problem of access to skills outside the formal educational system at the level of artisan training, is illustrated by the following statistic. Of the 25,000 new apprenticeship contracts registered in South Africa in 1983 and 1984, nearly 20,000 were for whites, while only 1,300 involved Africans. Some of this differential is related to the backlog of formal educational deficiencies, but a good deal is attributable to continuing racial discrimination in various industries.

Segregated facilities with large differences in the resources set aside for each racial group have existed in South Africa for centuries. Education, including the language of instruction, has always been a critical issue. Insistence on the use of English in white schools after the Anglo-Boer War was a fundamental concern of Afrikaner nationalists. The Afrikaner leadership of the National Party saw education as a key to development and advancement not only of individuals but of Afrikaners as a group. Educational "reform" in the guise of the Bantu Education Act was designed to provide Africans with a level and content of education that would be consistent with their role as menial servants in the overall society. The South African government's 1986 declaration that the "alternative" educational structures that had been springing up in the black townships were illegal is indicative of its continued belief in the power of education to change the individual and his or her role in society.

Access to education has been extremely unequal by race. Even the relatively dramatic quantitative measures of its differential availability (the number of pupils in school, expenditures per pupil, staffing ratios) understate the degree to which education for Africans, and to a somewhat lesser extent for coloreds and Asians, has lagged behind that available for whites. As recently as 1984 the number of Africans in their final year of secondary school was only 60 percent as high as the number of whites, although there were six to seven times as many Africans as whites in the same age-group. Dropout rates for Africans at all levels of primary and secondary school are high. The 1984 dropout rates showed that only 36 percent of African pupils starting primary school could be expected to complete secondary school.[9] Furthermore, the historical neglect of African education leaves a "pipeline" of children in school that is only a fraction of those eligible. The combination of all these factors meant that in 1984 some 20 percent *more* whites than Africans passed their matriculation examination at the end of secondary school, notwithstanding the vastly larger numbers of Africans of secondary school age.

The neglect will take a long time to fix. The increased resources the South African government has begun to provide for the education of all persons of color will affect the incomes of Africans only some years hence. How to deal with the realities of educational inequality and related skill shortages and income differentials in the meantime is a major question.

The data in Table 2.4 give one indication of the lag in investment in education for Africans relative to whites in South Africa and reflect the strategy of the National Party in its first two decades of rule. One of the key elements in developing an educa-

TABLE 2.4. SCHOOL ENROLLMENT DATA, 1945–1970

*Enrollment in teacher training colleges
and in upper and lower secondary schools*

Year	Teacher training colleges		Two-year upper secondary schools*		Three-year lower secondary schools†	
	White	African	White	African	White	African
1945	2,381	5,382	23,178	919	96,067	11,706
1955	5,238	5,899	31,949	2,067	133,612	32,916
1960	7,752	4,292	48,088	2,576	166,978	45,505
1965	10,209	4,548	na	na	na	na
1970	11,441	7,548	82,248	9,115	213,120	113,374

Sources: Republic of South Africa, *Statistical Yearbooks,* 1964 and 1974.

Note: na = not available.
* Standards 9 and 10 for whites, 4 and 5 for Africans.
† Standards 6–8 for whites, 1–3 for Africans.

tional system is training teachers. The figures show clearly that the number of Africans in teacher training was either constant or falling for twenty years. A slump occurred, for example, following the introduction of Bantu education in the mid-1950s. Investment in white education grew very rapidly, however, and the National Party's accomplishments are evident in the teacher training figures. By the mid-1950s, although South Africa had three to four times as many African as white citizens (and an even higher ratio among school-age children), more whites than Africans were being trained as teachers. The small numbers of Africans reaching lower or upper levels of secondary school are also indicative of the size of the education lag. In 1945 almost 25 times as many whites as Africans were in their final two years of secondary school; by 1970 this ratio had dropped to 9 : 1. The figures are slightly less dramatic at the lower secondary school level: the ratio declined from about 8 : 1 to 2 : 1 between 1945 and 1970. The differential educational attainment of the older and most experienced members of the work force illustrates some of the continuing source of wage and income differentials between whites and Africans.

In the election campaign of 1948, the National Party promised a major dismantling of what little had been done in the past to further African education. Once elected, the new government's leaders made good their pledge. The Bantu Education

Act brought all schools—public or private, sectarian or religious—under government control, and required the use of the Bantu education curriculum. It placed universities that had been established mainly for the education of blacks under government control, established new black universities, prohibited whites from attending universities designated for blacks, and made enrollment of blacks at white universities subject to government control. Church-sponsored schools could no longer provide leadership training to black South Africans or, indeed, Africans from other parts of the continent: in order to continue operating, these schools had to conform to the Bantu curriculum. For two to three decades, black education not only failed to advance but actually lost ground.

In brief, racial discrimination, by custom and law, has deprived the majority of South Africa's population of access to almost every mechanism by which most people in a society gain a share in economic development. Ownership of land and natural resources, as well as permission to conduct business, was prohibited or was available only on application; access to education and training was restricted; and higher-skilled jobs for those with adequate training were put out of reach by the color bar. At the same time, whites, particularly Afrikaners in the post–World War II era, were put at an advantage, including being paid well above a "market-clearing" wage for unskilled work. Systematic evidence is lacking only for the restricted access of blacks to capital markets or to the acquisition of financial assets. However, in light of discrimination in ownership of assets that could provide collateral for loans and in issuance of trading licenses, and considering the low levels of wage income and education, it is hardly surprising to find little evidence of significant financial asset ownership among South Africa's black communities. The principal exceptions may be in ownership of life insurance policies and in assets owned by the Asian community, particularly in Natal.

Discrimination and Income Distribution

How have these tendencies toward discrimination in access influenced the distribution of South Africa's national income over time? Numerous studies have examined racial differences in income. The easiest to do and to understand are those based on wage comparisons in the same industry or geographic area.

The longest series available on relative wage rates is for gold mining, an industry of fundamental political and economic importance. Figure 2.2 illustrates the pattern of real wages for white and African workers, and the ratio of white to African wages, from 1911 to 1985. (See also Appendix Table C.) Between 1911 and the end of World War II, real wages of miners in both racial groups first declined and then recovered—though the decline was smaller and the recovery better for whites than for Africans. Following the introduction of the civilized labor policy in the 1920s, the ratio of white to African wages rose steadily, from 11 : 1 in 1926 to 13 : 1 in 1946. Then, for nearly twenty years African real wages were almost unchanged; they began to rise only in the mid-1960s, and in 1970 were only 16 percent above

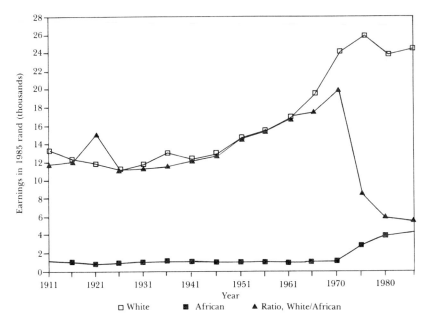

Sources: For 1911–1966, F. Wilson, *Labour in South African Gold Mines 1911–1969* (London: Cambridge University Press, 1972), 66. For 1970–1980, Republic of South Africa, *South African Statistics, 1982.* For 1985, C. Cooper et al., *Race Relations* (Johannesburg: South African Institute of Race Relations, 1986), citing South African Statistical Services.

FIG. 2.2. RELATIVE WAGES IN SOUTH AFRICAN GOLD MINES, 1911–1985

the 1946 level. Meanwhile, real white wages rose by 87 percent over the same period, increasing the ratio to 20:1. The period 1970–1985 saw a remarkable shift: white real wages in the mines were only fractionally higher in 1985 than in 1970, while African wages had risen by 250 percent. The largest increase came in the first half of the 1970s in response to the rise in the dollar gold price, waves of African labor unrest, and what the mining companies perceived as a shortage of African labor. Nonetheless, the ratio of white to African wages in the mines was still 6:1 in 1985, reflecting in part the remnants of the color bar. It was still illegal for African mine workers to obtain a blasting license, a restriction that limited their advancement regardless of ability.

Other major sectors of the economy show similar patterns of a widening wage gap between whites and Africans up to 1970 and then a decline for fifteen years, as shown in Figure 2.3. (See also Appendix Table D.) The ratios have not been as high in the nonmining sectors for a variety of reasons, such as different applications of the color bar and different skill mixes among whites and blacks. As the data in Appendix Table D also show, the gap has always been much smaller for colored and, especially, for Asian workers than for Africans, and the pattern of increasing differentials until 1970 followed by declines to 1985 holds in almost every case. The early 1970s represented something of a watershed in relative positions of white and black wage rates, though the wage differentials in favor of whites were still quite large by 1985: 2.8:1 for colored workers, 2.0:1 for Asian workers, and 3.8:1 for African workers.

The more complex studies of income distribution attempt to allocate all of South Africa's income on the basis of race. More than three dozen such efforts, using various definitions of income, have been carried out for years stretching from 1917 to 1985, and their results are summarized in Table 2.5. Once one moves from wages to total income as the base of comparison, the differentials become considerably wider: physical and financial asset ownership is even more highly concentrated in white hands than is the distribution of education and skills; whites benefit from differential access to employment as well. A higher dependency ratio in the black communities is also part of the explana-

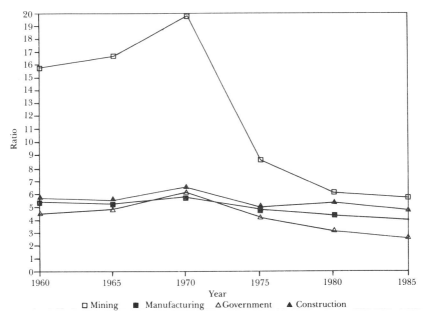

Sources: Calculated from employment and earnings data in Republic of South Africa, *South African Statistics*, 1976 and 1982, and *Bulletin of Statistics*, December 1986.

FIG. 2.3.   WAGE RATIO, WHITE TO AFRICAN, BY SECTOR, 1960–1985

tion. In 1985, for example, while whites enjoyed a *wage* ratio relative to colored, Asian, and African workers of 2.8:1, 2.0:1, and 3.8:1, the *per capita income* advantage was 4.3:1, 3.4:1 and 8.9:1, respectively.

The data on overall income distribution are sufficiently crude that one should not try to read too much into any small differences. Nevertheless, they indicate a pattern consistent with the story of South Africa's overall development. Broadly speaking, whites' share of total income in South Africa has always been very large relative to their proportion of the total population. The white share of income dropped from 75 percent in 1917 to under 60 percent in 1985, changing most dramatically after 1970. The 1970s saw the rapid increase in the international price of gold, a decline in the recruitment of black mine workers from outside South Africa, a wave of black labor unrest early in the decade, intensified international pressure on South Africa for increases in wages for blacks, and substantial increases in real black wages. The result was a substantial shift in the overall

TABLE 2.5. MEASURES OF INCOME DISTRIBUTION, 1917–1985*

Year	White	Colored	Asian	African	Black	Total
			Percentage of total income received			
1917	75.0	na	na	na	25.0	100.0
1924	75.2	5.3	1.6	17.9	24.8	100.0
1936	74.9	4.5	1.9	18.7	25.1	100.0
1946	73.6	4.3	1.9	20.2	26.1	100.0
1956	72.6	5.2	2.1	20.1	27.4	100.0
1960	72.3	5.0	1.9	20.8	27.7	100.0
1970	71.9	5.9	2.2	20.0	28.1	100.0
1980	60.8	7.4	2.9	28.9	39.2	100.0
1985	56.8	7.8	3.1	32.3	43.2	100.0
			Per capita income relative to overall average			
1917	3.5	na	na	na	0.32	1.00
1924	3.4	0.68	0.67	0.26	0.32	1.00
1936	3.6	0.56	0.83	0.27	0.32	1.00
1946	3.5	0.53	0.76	0.29	0.33	1.00
1956	3.5	0.56	0.70	0.30	0.34	1.00
1960	3.7	0.53	0.63	0.30	0.34	1.00
1970	4.2	0.64	0.76	0.28	0.34	1.00
1980	3.9	0.83	1.04	0.40	0.46	1.00
1985	3.9	0.91	1.15	0.44	0.51	1.00
			Per capita income relative to African income			
1917	na	na	na	na	na	na
1924	12.9	2.6	2.5	1.0	1.2	3.8
1936	13.2	2.1	3.0	1.0	1.2	3.7
1946	12.0	1.8	2.6	1.0	1.1	3.4
1956	11.8	1.9	2.3	1.0	1.2	3.3
1960	12.4	1.8	2.1	1.0	1.1	3.3
1970	14.9	2.3	2.7	1.0	1.2	3.5
1980	10.0	2.1	2.6	1.0	1.2	2.5
1985	8.9	2.1	2.6	1.0	1.2	2.3

Sources: Most of the data are taken from the invaluable summary of 40 studies of income distribution by Stephen Devereaux, *South African Income Distribution 1900–1980* (Cape Town: Southern African Labour and Development Research Unit, 1984).

Note: na = not available.

* Income concepts are mixed in different studies, and each figure reported is an average of data from several sources, sometimes for more than one year around the year referred to.

distribution of income away from whites toward all black groups, and some narrowing of the differentials by race. Nonetheless, by 1985 the per capita white income was still three to four times those of Asian and colored South Africans, and nine times that of Africans. The skewing of income to whites puts South Africa among the countries with the most unequal distribution of income.

Other observations may be noteworthy. The relative income position of whites improved during two periods when government policy explicitly favored them. The first was in the 1920s and 1930s, when the civilized labor policy absorbed poor whites at higher wages at the expense of blacks. The second occurred in the period from the 1950s through 1970, when the National Party's apartheid strategy was combined with substantial economic growth. The relative positions among Asians, coloreds, and Africans in South Africa were fairly stable. One might speculate that the declining position of Asians and coloreds relative to whites between World War II and 1960 reflected the implementation of National Party policy, while their improvement in relative terms during the 1960s reflected their greater ability to beat the color bar as economic growth put pressure on the supply of skilled white labor. In any case, the data seem to support what one would expect to find: the early domination of the white share, its decline over time, and some important episodic changes that reflected distinctive phases of government policy or of economic growth.[10]

In addition to data on the distribution of income by race, some information is available on the size distribution of income. Some variant of this measure is generally used when one talks of income inequality. In a comprehensive review of the evidence in the mid-1970s, Michael McGrath reached a number of interesting and important conclusions.[11] First, he suggests that on the most commonly used measure of inequality (the Gini coefficient), South Africa's income distribution is at least as unequal as that of any country in the world, though at 0.68 it is not far from some other extreme cases (Brazil, Mexico, and Sierra Leone at 0.61, and Honduras at 0.63). Of greater interest, perhaps, is the finding that *within* the various racial groups in South Africa, the distribution is least unequal, or most equal, among whites. The reason is simple. The objective of South African governments since the 1920s, especially since the National Party came to power, has been to eliminate the class of poor whites. The civilized labor policy and all its successors put a floor under white incomes at the expense of blacks. The result is that the bottom end of the income distribution has been all but eliminated for white South Africans. It is often the large concentration of people at the bottom that provides extreme inequality according to Gini coefficients or any other measure.

McGrath found that income distributions are more unequal among colored, Asian, and African households than among white households. This is because those lucky enough to get a modern-sector job are almost by definition put into a *relatively* good position within their racial group. The changes in wage rates that have taken place since 1975, combined with the effects of the recession of the 1980s, have probably increased the inequality within racial groups, particularly among Africans, who suffer the greatest unemployment. An increasing polarization of the black communities along economic lines has been going on for a decade or more. It can be expected to persist if past economic and political reform policy is continued. The only mitigating factor is that intrafamily transfer payments may have led to some "trickle-down" of wage increases to the less fortunate family members.

A final word of caution is needed about interpretation. The evidence represents, at best, measures of cash and in-kind income received by the population. In any country, one might question whether money buys happiness. In South Africa, the legal and institutional framework makes this question even more important. Most African employees are either migrants, living for long periods away from their families, or commuters, moving daily or weekly over relatively long distances.[12] The income figures given here refer to gross income differentials. They take no account of the cost of earning income; of the provision of income in kind at subsidized rates, such as for housing for black or white mine workers; or of the differential access by workers' racial group to accommodation near their families. Nor, of course, do they reflect any of the other costs inherent in being on the bottom, or benefits of being on the top, in a society dominated by racial differences.

THE HOMELANDS

The homelands policy of the National Party has been a key element in the policy of grand apartheid. The Nationalists took the notion of the Native Reserves, which had existed since 1913, to the extreme and planned to keep them as labor reservoirs for white employers in South Africa. But after two decades, it became increasingly clear that the economic basis of this policy had to change. Employment opportunities had to be expanded within the homelands, not just in areas adjacent to them. As a result of the South African government's preoccupation with the homelands, it has collected statistics on them for some time, and this makes it possible to examine what has been happening there.

Some basic data on the homelands and the rest of South Africa are provided in Table 2.6 and Table 2.7. In 1985, 75 percent of the total population was African and therefore technically allocated to one of the ten homelands. Of South Africa's 21.4 million Africans, 14 million were permanently living in the homelands. Another 1.5 million were living as migrant laborers, without their families, elsewhere in the country, but were permanently "domiciled" in the homelands. The remaining 5.9 million were more or less permanently resident in the white areas of South Africa, on farms or in segregated townships around the urban areas. Approximately 9 million Africans had lost their South African citizenship with the "independence" of Bophuthatswana, Ciskei, Transkei, and Venda. Some 4 million of these were living, either settled or as migrants, in white areas.

The percentage of South Africa's total population living in the homelands increased from 33 percent to 42 percent between 1970 and 1985, in part because of the more rapid rates of natural increase among the African population and redefinition of areas, but also because of the forced removals of blacks from white farms and urban centers. Estimates vary, but possibly

TABLE 2.6. BASIC DATA: THE HOMELANDS AND WHITE AREAS
OF SOUTH AFRICA, 1985

Region	Area (000 km²)	Arable land (hectare)	Population (000)	Absent workers (000)	GDP (R mn)	GNP (R mn)
Bophuthatswana	40.5	400	1,721	362	1,163	2,640
Ciskei	7.8	75	750	108	397	825
Gazankulu	6.6	65	620	75	230	530
KaNgwane	3.8	36	448	109	108	485
KwaNdebele	0.9	24	286	92	52	411
KwaZulu	31.0	565	4,382	770	1,062	4,044
Lebowa	21.8	347	2,157	283	540	1,604
Qwaqwa	0.6	7	209	60	110	363
Transkei	42.0	754	3,000	412	1,359	2,909
Venda	6.9	65	460	51	245	446
Total homelands	161.9	2,338	14,033	2,322	5,266	14,257
White areas	1,059.2	12,260	19,477	—	104,338	89,992
South Africa	1,221.1	14,598	33,510	—	109,604	104,249

Sources: For arable land, Michael Cobbett, "Agriculture in South Africa's Homelands,"
paper presented at York University, York, UK, 1986. All other data from
Development Bank of Southern Africa, *Annual Report, 1985–86* (Pretoria).

Note: Population is de facto. Migrant workers are included in the total for white areas.
Other citizens of the homelands permanently resident in white areas are included
in the figures for white areas rather than for the homelands. Absent workers are
the sum of migrant workers in white areas and those who live in the homelands
and commute daily or weekly to white areas for employment.

TABLE 2.7. HOMELANDS' PERCENTAGE CONTRIBUTION TO
SOUTH AFRICAN ECONOMY, VARIOUS MEASURES, 1970–1985

Measure	1970	1980	1985
Total land	13.3	13.3	13.3
Arable land	16.0	16.0	16.0
Population	32.7	39.1	41.9
GDP	2.4	3.8	4.8
GNP	8.8	10.2	13.7
Government expenditure	na*	9.3	12.4
Agricultural GDP	7.5	10.8	9.8

Sources: For 1970, T. Malan and P. S. Hattingh, *Black Homelands in South Africa* (Pretoria:
Africa Institute of South Africa, 1976). For 1980 and 1985, calculated from
Development Bank of Southern Africa, *Annual Report, 1985–86* (Pretoria).

Note: na = not available.
* Data are not available on a comparable definition because of differences in sources
between 1970 and later years.

20–25 percent of the 1985 population in the homelands had arrived there as a part of direct government action.[13]

Economic Activity

The homelands' productivity can be gauged from the distribution of GDP (the value of income generated, or final goods produced, *within* a given geographic area). As Table 2.7 indicates, the aggregate of all ten homelands produced 4.8 percent of South Africa's total GDP in 1985. While this was twice the 2.4 percent share produced in 1970, it does not nearly match the homelands' 42 percent share of the total population. The source of the increase in GDP also bears comment. With the growing recognition in the 1970s of the political and economic failure of the homelands policy, the government began to make large increases in the allocations of expenditure to the homelands. In 1970 expenditures by or on behalf of the homeland governments were only R90 million. The total expanded to R1.4 billion in 1980 and R4.7 billion in 1985. As a share of homelands' GDP, this sum represented an increase from 31 percent to 89 percent (see Table 2.8). Since the wages and salaries paid to government employees in the homelands form a part of measured GDP, the lion's share of the measured growth in homelands' GDP between 1970 and 1985 represented higher government salary payments, not increased production of goods and marketable services, and they were financed primarily by transfers from the central government, not from taxes on productive local activities.[14] The deficits of the homeland governments were 15 percent of homeland GDP in 1985, and transfers of Customs Union revenues from the central government equivalent to another 14 percent were included in their revenue.

The status of the homelands as labor reserves is illustrated by several types of data. The number of workers domiciled in the homelands but working as migrants or commuting to jobs in white areas of South Africa rose from nearly 1.5 million to over 2.3 million between 1970 and 1985. The percentage of the total population "absent" from the homelands for purposes of work decreased from over 30 percent in 1970 to nearly 17 percent in 1986. Several factors contributed to this decline: the growth of

TABLE 2.8. ECONOMIC STRUCTURE: THE HOMELANDS AND WHITE AREAS OF SOUTH AFRICA, 1970–1985

Year	Homelands	White areas	South Africa
	Agriculture as % of GDP		
1970	25.1	7.7	8.1
1980	19.5	6.5	7.0
1985	10.7	5.0	5.2
	Agriculture as % of GNP		
1970	7.3	8.6	8.5
1980	7.7	7.3	7.3
1985	4.0	5.8	5.5
	GNP as % of GDP		
1970	346	90	96
1980	252	89	95
1985	271	86	95
	Government expenditure as % of GDP		
1970	30.8	na*	na*
1980	62.5	24.4	25.9
1985	88.7	31.6	34.4

Sources: For 1970, calculated from T. Malan and P. S. Hattingh, *Black Homelands in South Africa* (Pretoria: Africa Institute of South Africa, 1976). For 1980 and 1985, calculated from Development Bank of Southern Africa, *Annual Report, 1985–86* (Pretoria).

Note: na = not available.
* Data are not available on a comparable basis of calculation for 1970.

the population by forced removals from white areas, natural increase in population and a rising share of children below working age in the total homelands population, rising unemployment, and the swelling numbers of government-sector jobs with homeland governments.

Gross national product (GNP) measures the income received, rather than income generated, in a geographic area. In the case of the homelands, the excess of GNP over GDP is represented principally by the income of commuters and the portion of migrants' income that is estimated to be sent back to the homeland. The effect of remittances and commuter earnings is illustrated by the homelands' contribution to South Africa's total GNP (see Table 2.7). The homelands' share rose from 8.8 percent to 13.7 percent of GNP between 1970 and 1985. This increase reflects several factors, including the rising wages of Africans relative to whites, the growth in the homelands' share of GDP (due largely to greater government employment there), and the increase in the share of the South African population living or domiciled in the homelands. While the effects of government policies aimed at decentralizing industry to the homeland areas undoubtedly had some measurable effect on the share of economic activity there, the factors just mentioned seem to be by far the most important in explaining the increase in the share of South Africa's GNP going to the homelands since 1970. Even with the large increase in the homelands' shares, average 1985 per capita GNP of the 19.5 million people of *all* races in white areas was five and one-half times that in the homelands.

Another way of looking at the importance of the homelands as labor reserves is by examining the ratio of their GNP to their GDP—that is, the ratio of income received by those domiciled in the homelands to the income actually generated by production there, including government employment funded by transfers. On the average, income from employment outside the homelands was about two and one-half times as important as income generated within the homelands in 1970, while even by 1985, despite the increase in government employment, it was still over one and one-half times as important (see Table 2.9). Again, much of the reason for the decline in migrant and commuter workers' incomes relative to GDP as a source of income is a reflection of the increased government-sector wage bill in the homelands, not of increased production of goods or services for sale.

The role of the agricultural sector within the homelands is worth special consideration. One might expect traditional agricultural activities to be an important actual and potential source of income for the black population of South Africa. The homelands hold a slightly larger percentage of arable land (or land suitable for crops) than of total land in South Africa (16 percent versus 13 percent); and some of the land is relatively fertile. However, as shown in Table 2.10, the arable land per capita, including all migrants and settled Africans, in white areas of South Africa is about 0.63 hectares, while in the homelands—

TABLE 2.9. ECONOMIC STRUCTURE: THE HOMELANDS AND
WHITE AREAS OF SOUTH AFRICA, 1985

Region	Absent workers as % of population	Agriculture as % of GDP	Government expenditure as % of GDP	GNP as % of GDP
Bophuthatswana	21.0	4.5	85.7	227
Ciskei	14.4	5.0	149.1	208
Gazankulu	12.1	10.4	88.3	230
KaNgwane	24.3	16.7	108.3	449
KwaNdebele	32.2	5.8	132.7	790
KwaZulu	17.6	19.6	79.6	381
Lebowa	13.1	8.3	81.1	297
Qwaqwa	28.7	3.6	137.3	330
Transkei	13.7	12.1	72.4	214
Venda	11.1	10.6	113.1	182
Total homelands	*16.5*	*10.7*	*88.7*	*271*
White areas	na	5.0	31.6	86
South Africa	na	5.2	34.4	95

Sources: Calculated from Development Bank of Southern Africa, *Annual Report,
1985–86* (Pretoria), and from Michael Cobbett, "Agriculture in South Africa's
Homelands," paper presented at York University, York, UK, 1986.

Note: na = not available

counting current residents and excluding migrants—it averages
only 0.17 hectares.[15] And it seems clear that overgrazing and
erosion are significantly greater problems in the homelands,
which means that productivity is lower even on land classified in
both areas as arable.

In 1985, agricultural production as a share of GDP in the
homelands was about 11 percent, down from 20 percent in 1980,
while in white areas of South Africa it was about 5 percent, down
from 7 percent in 1980. Agricultural output per capita in the
homelands in both years was only 15 percent of that in the rest of
South Africa. What about the productivity of land? In 1985,
agricultural GDP per hectare of arable land was about half in the
homelands what it was in white areas. Thus, even if agricultural
productivity per arable hectare in the homelands could be doubled, and raised to the same level of that in white areas of the
country, it would add only 10 percent to the GDP in the homelands, and less than 5 percent to the income of Africans resident

TABLE 2.10. COMPARATIVE DATA: THE HOMELANDS AND
SOUTH AFRICA, 1985

Region	GDP per capita (rand)	GNP per capita* (rand)	Arable land per capita (hectare)	GNP per capita as % of South African GNP per capita
Bophuthatswana	676	1,342	0.23	43.1
Ciskei	529	1,019	0.10	32.7
Gazankulu	371	774	0.10	24.9
KaNgwane	241	951	0.08	30.6
KwaNdebele	182	1,148	0.08	36.9
KwaZulu	242	862	0.13	27.7
Lebowa	250	679	0.16	21.8
Qwaqwa	526	1,365	0.03	43.9
Transkei	453	853	0.25	27.4
Venda	533	883	0.14	28.4
Total homelands	*375*	*916*	*0.17*	*29.4*
White areas	5,357	5,015	0.63	161.2
South Africa	3,271	3,111	0.44	100.0

Sources: Calculated from Development Bank of Southern Africa, *Annual Report,* *1985–86* (Pretoria), and from Michael Cobbett, "Agriculture in South Africa's Homelands," paper presented at York University, York, UK, 1986.

* Migrant workers are counted in the denominator of the homelands and are excluded from the denominator of white areas.

or domiciled there. This raises major questions about future economic development strategies for any government in South Africa. It also suggests that the notion that the homelands are basically traditional, rural, agricultural areas—a belief held by many people—is well off the mark.[16]

Government Programs

As the South African government reappraised its homeland development policies in the 1970s, it focused on three elements for improving economic conditions. First, it increased expenditures through the homeland governments to improve social and physical infrastructure. Second, it tried to induce the private sector to locate a growing share of its activities in the homelands, or in areas immediately adjacent to them, in order to provide increased employment for homeland citizens. Finally, it introduced a development banking institution to provide funds and technical assistance on a World Bank model as a complement to the other two parts of the program.

The effect of increased government expenditure in the homelands has already been discussed, and the numbers involved are very large indeed. The budgets of the homeland governments alone expanded from a negligible share to 13 percent of total South African government expenditure by 1985. The program of "decentralization incentives" for regional development, both in the homelands and in areas of South Africa outside of the main economic centers, was substantially enhanced in 1982. The following example illustrates the new incentive package. A firm choosing to operate in the homeland of Qwaqwa would be entitled to a rebate of 40 percent of any railage costs of materials and equipment, 95 percent of its total wage bill up to a maximum of R110 per worker per month for seven years, a training grant, a 75 percent subsidy on rent and interest payments for ten years, a 40 percent subsidy on the interest rate on money used to build housing, up to R500,000 in relocation costs if coming from a more developed area in South Africa, and a 10 percent price preference on government tenders.[17] Such a firm would also, of course, be able to apply to the Board of Trade and Industry for tariff protection or for rebates or remission of import duties on imported inputs. Such incentives have resulted in a substantial amount of investment in the homelands and other decentralization areas, with the government picking up the bill for some of the capital costs and a substantial portion of the operating costs of projects.

In the first three years of the reformulated incentive program the government announced approval of schemes with investment of nearly R5 billion; creation of over 200,000 jobs could be expected when the projects were complete. Budgetary expenditures from 1983–1984 to 1985–1986 were expected to be over R1 billion. Since most of the incentives are operating—not capital—subsidies, the amounts will expand as projects are undertaken and will remain as budgetary costs for seven to ten years. No data exist on the completion of projects or their actual employment effect; but the employment subsidy alone, at over R1,200 per job per year, would cost nearly R250 million annually for seven years for the schemes approved from 1982 to 1985.[18]

It is important to recognize that the expenditures undertaken for this strategy do *not* result in new economic activity within South Africa; they simply shift the activity from one part of the country to another. No net contribution accrues to GDP. Indeed, if foreign investors took up the incentives, the profits that they took out of the country could exceed the real contribution to South Africa's GDP.[19] The value of real national income from this package of incentives then would decline, not increase.

The Development Bank of Southern Africa, established in 1981, replaced the Corporation for Economic Development, whose function was to promote development in the homelands. The Development Bank has a broader mandate than its predecessor and has taken on a role of technical assistance and planning, as well as investment, in a wide array of projects. These range from road and irrigation infrastructure through electricity projects, small-business development, agriculture, industry, and urban development. The bank's operations increased rapidly. By March 1986 it had already committed to finance 234 projects, with a total expenditure of R1.8 billion, and was expecting to enter into another 218 projects, with a total expenditure of nearly R2 billion. Funds have so far come from the South African government or been raised on the country's capital markets, but the intention of the bank is to raise funds from international markets as well. Apart from its technical assistance and planning activities, the bank appears to aim entirely at "bankable" projects, unlike some of the general government programs. It also has taken a regional approach that goes beyond the artificial boundaries of the homelands.

The South African government has made extremely large new commitments of funds to homeland development in the past decade or more. Some of these—for education, health services, physical infrastructure—will contribute to the long-term development of South Africa and to its African citizens. Others—like the decentralization incentives, the growth of homeland bureaucracies that duplicate other services or that simply provide sinecure jobs—are a drain on resources that could be invested more productively. The amounts involved were large enough to make some difference to black South

Africans. For example, in 1985 some R4.7 billion went to home-land government expenditures, R500 million went for decentral-ization incentives, and R1–R2 billion of investment came through the Development Bank—a total of over $3 billion. Given the government's policies, however, the positive impact of such expenditures is very limited.

THE MIGRANT LABOR SYSTEM AND THE DISTRIBUTION OF ECONOMIC BENEFITS

The system of migrant labor and controls on the movements of black South Africans, an economic and sociopolitical mechanism over the black population that is more than a century old, has had a fundamental effect on all aspects of South Africa's society and economy. The system depends on the combination of a lack of economic alternatives for black workers, especially those domi-ciled in homelands, and control of movement of blacks to and within white areas of the country. Its effects also depend on other factors, especially the policies on job reservation, education and training, and settlement by black workers. As a result, rather than a free market for labor, South Africa has a series of seg-mented markets, sustained by a full range of segregation instru-ments. For many decades the effect was to raise artificially the demand for—and price of—white labor at all skill levels and to depress artificially the demand for—and price of—black labor. The reduced price of black labor at higher skill levels came from job reservation and restricted access to training. At lower skill levels, notably in agriculture, it came from the exceptionally poor alternative income-earning opportunities for blacks, particularly Africans in the homelands.

In the early years of the diamond and gold booms, the demand for labor was so great that, to avoid competitive bidding for African labor, the mining companies decided to combine forces in joint recruiting efforts. As in other parts of Africa during the colonial period, taxes were imposed on the indige-nous population; the need to pay taxes required them to work in the wage economy, thus inducing a supply of labor. A major cooperative effort was made to recruit for the gold mines from outside South Africa and to recruit widely enough throughout southern Africa that demand would not bid up the wage rate.

With the full development of the apartheid system after 1948, three elements of policy—the homelands concept, economic discrimination in favor of whites, and the migrant labor system—were linked and institutionalized in a highly formal way. Under the Nationalists, legalized job reservation became more extensive than it had been in the past. And millions of black South Africans were relocated to the homelands, many from white farming areas where the number of blacks a farmer could have on his land was limited.

By 1984, of the approximately 2.7 million African workers registered under the Black Labor Act in white areas of the country, 56 percent were migrants or commuters, either from a homeland or from a neighboring country. About 80 percent of the registered migrants from other countries were engaged in mining, compared with only 15 percent of those from South Africa.[20] South Africans represented over 95 percent of the migrant labor in all sectors except mining, where they were about 63 percent.

As the black labor force increased, and as the demand for labor in white areas and in almost all sectors of the economy grew during the post–World War II economic boom, the stresses on the system began to be felt in purely economic terms. The scale of movement of people was enormous. The time involved in commuting or in annual trips over large distances caused economic losses both to the individual employed and, often, to the employer. Subsidies were needed on the long commuter routes created by the decision to separate black residential areas from white residential, commercial, and industrial areas. Productivity suffered because of the conditions under which black migrants and commuters had to work. Lack of labor mobility geographically and between industries hampered reallocation from contracting to expanding industries. And the introduction of Bantu education had reduced the potential supply of trained people from the majority of the population.

The migrant labor system has had obvious economic benefits to some white areas of South Africa, but the nature of these benefits has changed over time, as has the nature of the beneficiaries. The system has had to work in tandem with other elements of control, particularly job reservation and influx control.[21]

The formation of the 1924 Pact government constituted a victory for white labor and Afrikaner farmers. Its programs skewed the demand for labor toward whites and limited the flow of black labor into all sectors except agriculture—thus assuring cheap labor to the farmers. The principal capitalist interests at the time were in mining, and the share holdings in the mines were substantially in foreign hands. The combination of wage policies, tariff protection, job reservation, and restrictions on movement of black workers effectively subsidized white agriculture and labor at the expense of mining interests and of the black population generally. Owners of manufacturing capital received protection and paid low black wages, but they also had to pay higher white wage rates and accept high ratios of white to black labor. During the quarter-century before 1948, the manufacturing sector had grown rapidly behind protection from tariffs, as well as from wartime isolation from markets, and had achieved considerable local participation. Also, ownership of the mining sector had shifted from foreign to domestic hands, and the South African mining houses were expanding their activities into the protected manufacturing sector. Before 1948, these domestic mining and manufacturing interests were predominantly from the English-speaking white community. Little love was lost between the mine and factory owners, on the one hand, and the Afrikaner working class and farmers, who were the principal constituents of the National Party, on the other. The program of promoting the economic interests of white agriculture and white labor with a healthy dose of Afrikaner nationalism culminated in the National Party election victory in 1948.

In the boom years of the 1950s and 1960s the system of control over the black population was further developed, and the preferences for whites were expanded. The effects can be seen clearly in the data reported earlier on relative wage levels and income distribution by race. During this period, it seems fairly clear, the controls on black labor, protection of manufacturing, and fairly orthodox fiscal and monetary policy produced a set of conditions that provided for rapid growth of income, increased rates of domestic saving, and high levels of capital investment. In the 1950s and 1960s the effects of influx control and the migrant labor system reduced the capital needs for growth by depressing the demand for infrastructure and housing—two heavy users of capital in all countries. The artificially high white wages and salaries were effectively subsidized by artificially low economic benefits—wages and salaries, infrastructure, and social services—provided to blacks.

By the 1970s the situation began to change substantially in several respects. The impact of the migrant labor system, and the other elements of control and discrimination, grew more ambiguous. The economic failure of the homelands was becoming clear. Shortages of skills were showing up in many sectors of the economy, and consequently the color bar was being eroded, especially by Asian and colored workers. The Bantu education system exacerbated the shortages of skills. Demands for wage increases and labor unrest were becoming less controllable. Forced removals increased the separation of job holders from their families and reduced the access of Africans to land, especially since many were moved from white farms where they had been able to raise some crops for their own use. The independence of the adjacent countries caused a rethinking of labor recruitment policies by the mining industry and by South Africa's neighbors. Labor recruitment from outside the country began to decrease in favor of domestic African workers.

During the early 1970s the dam broke on black wage levels, and, while still well below those of whites, black wages increased substantially in the 1970s and 1980s. The government recognized the need for a fundamental reconsideration of labor policies and, following some tentative changes in the early 1970s, appointed two commissions (Riekert and Wiehahn) to investigate manpower utilization and labor legislation. Both recommended substantial changes in legislation to remove the color bar and to open up access to jobs and to training. The major mining houses began to talk of the desirability of a "settled" black labor force. The government itself joined the practice of increasing black wages more rapidly than white wages, even though both the government and parastatals retained various forms of job preference for whites. Major parts of the influx control system were eliminated, making it possible for Africans who were not citizens of the homelands to move to urban areas, although not to white neighborhoods, since the Group Areas Act remained law.

The migrant labor system and several related elements of control were still in place in the late 1980s, but some basic conditions had changed substantially since 1970. Movement was underway both in and outside the mining sector to "stabilize" the black labor force. The vast improvement in black wages, which created larger income differentials within the black community, especially between rural and urban areas, was particularly important. The improvement in black per capita income came mainly from wage increases for those already employed rather than from expanded access of black workers to modern-sector jobs. These income differentials were exacerbated by the rapid rise in black unemployment during the 1984–1986 recession. More money was going into the homelands to create jobs, but the bulk of the jobs were in the government sector and therefore dependent on continued transfers from the central government. Since little improvement had been made in the homelands' agricultural sectors, and since the land scarcity continued to grow, the alternatives for those who failed to find modern-sector jobs by migrating or commuting were dismal. Access to both rural and urban land and to capital remained highly restricted, especially for Africans. Working for someone else, rather than self-employment, remained the only reasonable option for the vast majority of Africans.

3

SOUTH AFRICA AND THE INTERNATIONAL ECONOMY

Throughout its history, South Africa's economy has been relatively open in terms of flows of goods, capital, and people. In its heavy reliance on the export of primary products from the mining sector, it shares with similar nations a relatively high ratio of imports and exports to GDP. South Africa also has been a participant in international capital markets since the discovery of diamonds at Kimberley in 1867. White immigration played a major role in the development of the gold mines in the late nineteenth and early twentieth century and has been a major factor in the development of the economy since then. Recruitment of black workers for the mines throughout southern Africa has been an important part of South Africa's relationship with its neighbors for nearly a century.

FOREIGN TRADE

The overall importance of foreign trade to the South African economy is indicated by the data in Table 3.1, which show the ratio of imports and of exports to GDP. The openness of the economy as measured by these ratios declined somewhat during the Great Depression and the post–World War II era, reflecting the increased import substitution that occurred in manufacturing and, more generally, the faster growth of the domestic market during those periods. The higher figure for exports in the late 1970s is largely the result of the gold price boom, though coal exports increased significantly as well. The lowest trade ratios were experienced at the bottom of the Great Depression

TABLE 3.1. IMPORTS AND EXPORTS AS PERCENTAGE OF GDP,
1912–1985

Period*	Exports	Imports	Total trade
1912	39.6	22.8	62.3
1920	31.4	33.5	64.9
1925	31.1	25.5	56.6
1930	26.9	23.6	50.5
1935	21.5	21.7	43.2
1940	32.7	21.2	53.9
1946–1950	28.6	35.0	63.6
1951–1955	32.7	32.5	65.2
1956–1960	32.9	27.9	60.8
1961–1965	30.3	24.7	55.0
1966–1970	25.8	24.6	50.4
1971–1975	26.7	27.0	53.7
1976–1980	32.8	26.6	59.4
1981–1985	28.5	25.5	54.0

Sources: For 1912–1940, Republic of South Africa, *South African Statistics*, 1976. For
1946–1985, South African Reserve Bank, *Quarterly Bulletin*, various issues.

Notes: Ratios are at current prices; GDP is at factor cost. Data for 1912–1940 include
goods only; those for later years include goods and nonfactor services.
* Data for 1946–1950 through 1981–1985 are five-year averages.

and just prior to the freeing of the international price of gold in
1971. In the short term, large changes in the exchange rate
between the rand and international currencies strongly affect
the measured ratio of imports and exports to GDP.

The pattern of trade on a commodity-by-commodity basis
often reveals much about the nature and structure of a country's
economy. The most striking finding regarding the commodity
composition of South Africa's exports is the early and continued
dominance of gold, both as a share of total exports and as a share
of GDP (see Figure 3.1 and Appendix Table E). Agricultural
commodities, principally food grains, fruits, and vegetables, are
still important, but manufactured exports have gained ground.
If smelted metals are excluded from the definition of manufactured exports, the significance of the manufacturing sector as an
export earner is lower in South Africa than in other upper-
middle-income countries. It would appear that South Africa has
fewer manufactured exports than the newly industrialized countries (NICs): Brazil, Hong Kong, Singapore, South Korea, and

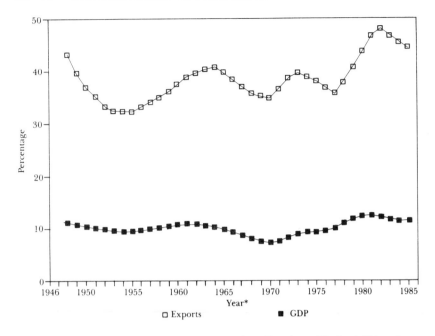

Sources: For 1912–1945, calculated from D. Hobart Houghton, *The South African Econ-
          omy*, 4th ed. (Capetown: Oxford University Press, 1976) and Republic of South
          Africa, *South African Statistics*, 1976. For 1946–1987, calculated from South
          African Reserve Bank, *Quarterly Bulletin*, various issues.

*Five-year averages, centered on middle year.

FIG. 3.1.   GOLD EXPORTS AS PERCENTAGE OF GDP AND OF VISIBLE
            EXPORTS*

even Yugoslavia. Furthermore, manufactured exports per capita
are lower in South Africa than in any of those countries except
Brazil.[1] A substantial portion of South Africa's manufactured
exports go to countries in southern Africa.

The pattern of import substitution in South Africa, a policy
that began in the early 1920s, has produced a marked change
in the commodity composition of imports. Some data for
1946–1985 are shown in Table 3.2. The rising shares of machinery and transport equipment, of oil and arms, and of chemicals
are matched by declining shares of semiprocessed raw materials
and most categories of manufactured goods, including consumer goods, metal products, food, beverages, and tobacco
products. The structure of industrial incentives in South Africa
generally provides protection for the final product through high

TABLE 3.2. PERCENTAGE DISTRIBUTION OF IMPORTS
BY MAJOR CATEGORY, 1946–1985

Year	Arms, oil, and misc.	Machinery and equipment	Chemicals	Other raw materials	Metal products	Food, beverages, and tobacco	Other manu- factured goods	Total
1946	4.2	19.8	4.7	6.7	10.0	13.5	41.2	100.0
1950	9.6	25.6	4.4	9.4	12.9	7.3	30.8	100.0
1955	8.9	31.8	6.9	7.3	10.1	5.4	29.6	100.0
1960	7.7	36.7	7.0	6.7	7.6	5.0	29.3	100.0
1965	7.0	42.1	7.1	7.5	11.0	7.0	18.3	100.0
1970	9.1	46.7	7.8	4.7	7.6	5.0	18.9	100.0
1975	18.6	43.7	7.6	5.9	8.3	3.7	12.2	100.0
1980	29.9	38.1	8.5	4.4	4.7	2.5	11.8	100.0
1985	17.9	40.5	12.1	4.6	5.1	4.8	15.0	100.0

Sources: Republic of South Africa, South African Statistics, Statistical Yearbook, and Bulletin of Statistics, various issues.

tariffs and quotas, but with low duties on imported intermediate goods and capital goods. This has biased industrial development in two ways. First, some tendency exists toward import intense use of raw materials and some intermediate goods in protected manufacturing. Second, the relatively low duty levels for capital goods have discouraged domestic production of investment goods. Both these biases make South Africa vulnerable to losses in foreign exchange earnings. The substantial drop in the quantity of imports over the most recent five-year period is due in large part to the decrease in domestic capital formation and a consequent decrease in the import of capital goods. The declining value of imports was also a result of falling oil prices. Neither change reflects a fundamental shift in the import intensity of the South African economy on a long-term basis.

Official statistics in South Africa no longer record the level of imports of crude oil, one of the few major raw materials that South Africa does not possess. The data from which Table 3.2 is drawn give a total of goods "not specified as to type"; these are mainly defense and petroleum imports. The effect of the first and second oil shocks and the Arab oil boycott is the primary reason this category rose from 9 percent of imports in 1970 to 30 percent in 1980, before dropping to 18 percent by 1985. Estimates of the exact level of oil imports vary considerably, as do estimates of the price premium that South Africa has had to pay since the Arab boycott began. If one takes a consensus estimate of 280,000 barrels per day consumption, with one-third of the consumption supplied by SASOL, imports for normal consumption purposes would be in the range of 70 million barrels per year. Depending on price, the total cost could range from $1 billion to over $2 billion annually, and it was probably even higher in 1979–1981. Imports for stockpiling would add to the bill. Since South Africa's normal imports in the last ten years have been running between $15 billion and $20 billion, oil represents at least 10–15 percent of the total import bill. With oil at $20 a barrel and gold at $400 an ounce, the annual oil bill is paid for by less than two months' gold exports. Since 1971, the dollar prices of oil and gold have tended to move in parallel.[2]

Opinion on the importance of South Africa's trade in strategic minerals varies greatly. While South Africa and southern Africa produce a large share of a wide range of minerals, their share of production of the key strategic minerals is relatively small in terms of both export earnings and the imports of the industrialized world. These minerals—chromium, manganese, cobalt (principally from Zaire and exported via the southern African rail system), and the platinum-group metals—are important in a broad spectrum of critical production activities for modern industry. Chromium is used for specialty steels; manganese in steel production of all kinds; cobalt for various high-stress purposes, such as jet engines; and the platinum-group metals as catalytic agents and in electronics.

It is easy either to minimize the effects of significant disruption or to overemphasize the vulnerability of Western economies to unavailability of these minerals. The importance of South Africa and the region as producers is such that any sudden disruption would have an immediate and dramatic effect on the markets. However, unlike oil, hard minerals can be stored fairly easily in quantities that are large relative to ordinary annual demand. Speculative buying in cobalt markets in response to concern about production capacity in Zaire during 1978 led to a severalfold increase in price over a period of a few months. With

all Western industrial economies and their steel sectors at historically very low levels of output in recent years, one could under-
estimate the effects of short-term supply disruptions. In the
short run, possibilities for substitution and recycling are limited,
and present stocks are low.

On the other hand, it is unrealistic to think of a situation in
which the Western economies would grind to a halt for a long
period because of unavailability of supplies. Estimates that have
been made of large declines in the GDP of Western countries in
response to a cutoff of minerals from southern Africa are based
on assumptions of *no* substitutability and limited recycling, assumptions that would not hold over periods of years. Further, the
Soviet-bloc countries are a major alternative supply source, and
the Soviet Union's response to past shortages of strategic materials suggests that it would act commercially and supply Western
demand, albeit at high prices. Because of limited short-run substitution, however, it would appear to be important for the Western industrial countries to maintain sufficient stocks of major
strategic minerals so that the markets would not panic in the
event of a dramatic short-run change in the availability of supplies from southern Africa.

Strategic minerals also impinge on the issue of the Western
industrial countries' imposing comprehensive mandatory economic sanctions against South Africa. A balanced reading of the
evidence suggests that the value of strategic minerals to South
Africa is relatively low (perhaps 10 percent of total exports), and
they are therefore not a major factor in South Africa's total
economy. But the strategic mineral question *is* of importance to
the West, as the exemption of minerals from the 1986 Comprehensive Anti-Apartheid Act, which imposed selective sanctions
against South Africa, demonstrates. However, its importance in
the long run should not be overestimated.

As an oil-importing, primary-product-exporting country,
South Africa might be expected to have suffered from declining
terms of trade since the early 1970s. Figure 3.2 shows two measures of the country's terms of trade: one inclusive and the other
exclusive of gold. It vividly demonstrates that without gold, the
long-term trend since World War II would have been against

South Africa, with a considerable fall—some 30 percent—since the first oil price increases of the mid-1970s. With gold, however, there is no downward long-term trend at all. The freeing of the gold price in 1971 meant that South Africa's terms of trade were substantially higher, on average, in the 1970s and 1980s than in the 1960s. Thus, the long-term slowdown of South Africa's growth rate that began in the 1960s was clearly not related to a general deterioration of the external terms of trade. Short-term changes in the gold price can have a major effect on macroeconomic management by the authorities, however. The increased gold price in 1986–1988 aided South Africa in adjusting to the effects of its debt standstill. The soft gold price in 1989 led to a significant set of pressures on domestic monetary, fiscal, and exchange rate policy in the past year.

CAPITAL FLOWS

Much has been written about the importance of foreign capital to South Africa, both historically and prospectively. Foreign

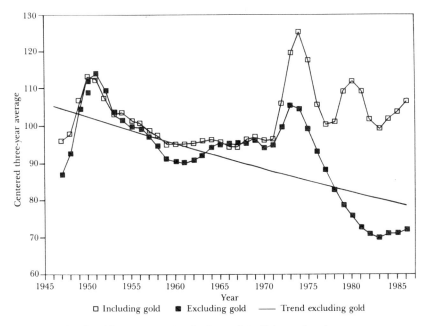

Source: South African Reserve Bank, *Quarterly Bulletin*, various issues.

FIG. 3.2. SOUTH AFRICAN TERMS OF TRADE, 1946–1987

investment has played an important role in South Africa's development since the early days of the diamond and gold mining industries. Frankel, for example, estimated that between 1870 and 1936, over £500 million ($10–$15 billion in today's prices) was invested in South Africa, mainly from British sources, financing between one-third and one-half of total capital formation.[3] Most of this capital went into the private sector, especially gold mining, where in the first half-century of the industry foreign capital provided about two-thirds of total investment. Gross capital inflow in financing the liabilities of South African governments and public utilities was also substantial, in excess of £200 million. By the 1930s over 40 percent of all British investment in Africa was in South Africa. Frankel makes the additional point that a substantial portion of the total gross investment by foreigners in South Africa represented reinvestment of their dividend earnings on shares and mining securities. Such reinvestment of earnings is the principal factor in the post–World War II increase in the value of direct foreign investment in South Africa.

One respect in which South Africa differs from other primary-product exporters (Chile is an extreme example in the opposite direction) is the extent to which it developed domestic sources of saving as well as domestic management and ownership in mining and manufacturing. In 1918, an estimated 82 percent of all mining dividends were paid abroad. Through the development of the South African mining houses and the increase in domestic capacity to save and invest, that figure was reduced to less than 50 percent by the end of World War II, and it continued to decline, dropping below 25 percent by the end of the 1960s.[4] While the *stock* of foreign investment in South Africa resulting from the early investments and from reinvestment of earnings is relatively large, the net *flow* of new foreign investment has been of declining importance.

The relative importance of net inflows of foreign investment of all kinds—public and private, direct and portfolio—is shown for the postwar years in Figure 3.3. (See also Appendix Table F.) From 1946 to 1950 the flow of foreign capital was very large, amounting to nearly 9 percent of GDP and financing over 31 percent of gross domestic investment. Since 1950, however, foreign capital has never financed more than 16 percent of domestic investment, and it has turned negative during several five-year periods. In short, the relatively large stock of foreign ownership in South Africa is not a result of substantial new investments in the past 30–40 years.

It is important to distinguish between direct and portfolio investment in South Africa. Direct investment takes the form of subsidiaries or joint ventures in which the foreign investor maintains a physical presence, employs workers directly, and pays taxes to the government. Foreign direct investment often involves the transfer of technology from home or office to local subsidiary or affiliate. However, the principal *financial* flows of foreign investment to South Africa for the past 30 years, as well as the flows that initially established the foreign ownership in the gold mines, have been portfolio investment. This is investment in listed securities of the public or private sector and, since the

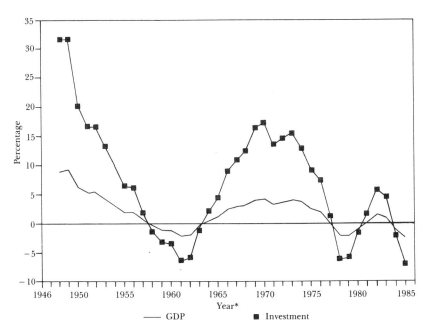

Source: South African Reserve Bank, national accounts tables.

*Five-year average, centered on middle year.

FIG. 3.3. NET FOREIGN CAPITAL INFLOW AS PERCENTAGE OF GDP AND OF GROSS DOMESTIC INVESTMENT, 1946–1987

1970s, in medium- and short-term bank loans that involve no direct ownership of production facilities. In principle, the flow of foreign capital has similar balance-of-payments effects and effects on external reserves, regardless of whether it is in the form of direct or portfolio investment.

Figure 3.4 shows the changing level and composition of South Africa's total foreign liabilities since the early 1960s. (See also Appendix Table G.) The lower two portions of each bar in the figure are fixed obligations, or debt, while the upper two portions represent direct or portfolio investment, mainly, though not exclusively, in equities. Several points are worth mentioning. First, public-sector borrowing by government and parastatals increased substantially over the period, chiefly in the 1970s. Second, short-term debt grew in relative importance through most of the period, especially after 1980, as the public sector had increasing difficulty borrowing in international markets for longer periods. Third, the value of private equity investment, in dollars at current prices, grew significantly in the 1970s but declined in the 1980s. Some of the changes are due to the varying exchange rate between the rand and the dollar. Changes in the exchange rate—*not* flows of funds—explain about a quarter of the increase in the dollar value of investments between 1978 and 1980, and virtually all of the decrease after 1980.

The pattern of foreign investment has changed markedly since 1956. At that time long-term equity investments represented over 75 percent of the total; by the mid-1980s foreign investment was dominated by debt, particularly short-term debt. Short-term debt alone accounted for over 40 percent of South Africa's liabilities to foreigners in 1985. This change occurred even though the total net foreign capital inflow over the period was very modest in relation to either GDP or domestic investment. Access to short-term credit has been South Africa's principal use of international finance since the late 1970s.

Frankel pointed out the importance of the reinvestment of dividend flows as new capital investment in South Africa prior to World War II. Similarly, the reinvestment of profits earned by foreign direct investors has been the main source of the expansion of their operations in the postwar years. The vast majority of

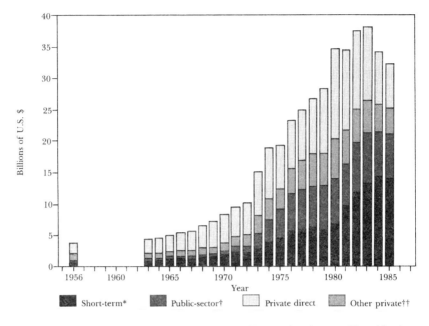

Sources: South African Reserve Bank, *Quarterly Bulletin*, various issues, tables of foreign liabilities, converted to dollars at year-end exchange rates.

* Includes both equity and debt.
† Includes both public authorities and parastatal corporations.
†† Includes both public- and private-sector liabilities due for payment within one year.

FIG. 3.4. LIABILITIES TO FOREIGNERS BY TYPE, 1956–1985

the increase in foreign direct investment, at least since the mid-1950s—when detailed statistics began to be published—and almost certainly longer, has involved the reinvestment of earnings of initial capital investment in South Africa, *not* new capital generated from sources outside the country.

The dominance of reinvested or retained earnings in the growth of total foreign direct investment since 1956 is shown in Figures 3.5 and 3.6. (See also Appendix Table H.) Even in the late 1950s undistributed profits represented about 60 percent of the value of total foreign direct investment, and by the early 1980s this share had grown to over 85 percent. Put differently, nearly 88 percent of the $11 billion increase in the value of foreign direct investment between 1956 and 1980 was due to reinvested or retained earnings, and less than 13 percent was due to new capital inflows from abroad. In current dollars the

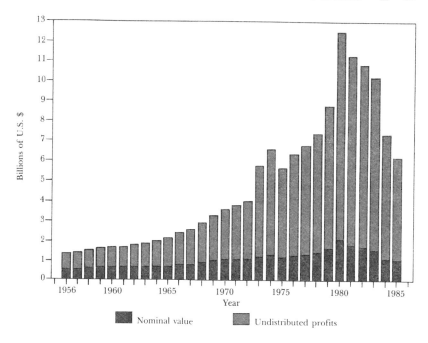

Source: South African Reserve Bank, *Quarterly Bulletin*, various issues, tables on foreign
liabilities converted to dollars at year-end exchange rates.

FIG. 3.5.   DIRECT EQUITY INVESTMENT IN CURRENT DOLLARS,
1956–1985

total value of direct equity investment in South Africa rose from
just over $1 billion in 1956 to a peak of over $12 billion in 1980,
and then fell with the decline in the rand to just over $6 billion in
1985. The value of the rand rose from $1.15 to $1.35 between
1978 and 1980, then declined to $0.39 by the end of 1985. An
alternative measure, the value of direct equity investment in
constant (1985) price rand is shown in Figure 3.6. Measured in
terms of real rand, the book value of direct equity investment in
South Africa peaked in the early 1970s and is now at the level of
the late 1960s. The comparison between the two figures suggests
that the large apparent increase in direct equity investment in
the 1970s was due to the combination of inflation and rand
appreciation relative to the dollar.

While profits reinvested in South Africa differ in some ways
from completely new investment, those profits could, of course,
have been repatriated. In that sense they are "new money" for

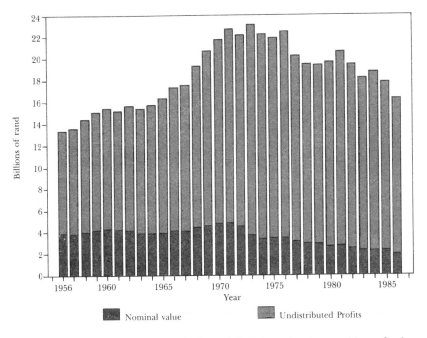

Nominal value   Undistributed Profits

Source: South African Reserve Bank, *Quarterly Bulletin*, various issues, tables on foreign
liabilities, deflated by implicit GDP deflator.

FIG. 3.6.   DIRECT EQUITY INVESTMENT IN 1985 RAND, 1956–1985

the South African economy. The relationships between the flows
of dividend and profit remittances, as shown in the balance of
payments, and the investment in equities for either direct or
portfolio investment for 1956–1985 are shown in Table 3.3 and
Figure 3.7. From a national financial viewpoint, the outward
flows of dividends, or investment flows in either direction, might
usefully be expressed in relation to the total export earnings;
those data are given in the table. The declining importance of
dividend or profit remittances relative to export earnings is
evident throughout the period and is a further indication of the
declining relative importance of foreign investment in South
Africa over the past three decades. Of greater interest, perhaps,
is the relative size of the dividend and profit outflows, on the one
hand, and the new investment inflows, on the other. Outflows of
dividends and profits have always exceeded inflows of capital,
including reinvested earnings. In the case of direct investment,
the dividend outflows have exceeded investment inflows by well

TABLE 3.3. PRIVATE LONG-TERM INVESTMENT FLOWS, AND
DIVIDENDS AND PROFITS, AS PERCENTAGE OF EXPORT EARNINGS,
1956–1985

Measure	1956–1965	1966–1975	1976–1985
Dividends and profits on direct investment	6.7	5.7	3.5
Long-term direct investment flows	0.8	2.7	0.6
Dividends and profits on all private direct and indirect investment	9.5	7.7	4.9
Long-term private direct and indirect investment	−1.4	6.4	0.2

Sources: Calculated from South African Reserve Bank, *Quarterly Bulletin,* various issues,
survey of foreign liabilities, balance-of-payments, and national accounts tables.

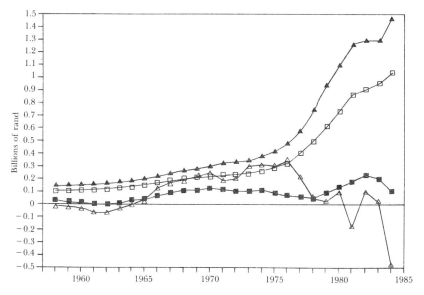

Dividends and branch profits of private investors earned on:
□ Foreign direct investment ▲ All private long-term investment
Investment flows of the private sector:
■ Foreign direct investment △ All private long-term investment

Source: South African Reserve Bank, *Quarterly Bulletin,* various issues, tables on foreign
liabilities, deflated by implicit GDP deflator.

Note: Five-year average, centered on middle year.

FIG. 3.7. PRIVATE LONG-TERM INVESTMENT AND
DIVIDEND PROFIT REMITTANCES

over three times since 1956. Indirect, or portfolio, investment is much more volatile than is the flow of direct investment, as the more erratic behavior of the total of direct plus indirect investment demonstrates. However, it is clear that for all private long-term investment—direct and portfolio—dividend and profit remittances have substantially exceeded capital inflows at least since 1956 and, according to Frankel's figures, for much longer.

What do these data imply about foreign investment and its effects on the South African economy? In the simplest terms, they suggest that, *if* all foreign investors gave up their present holdings in South Africa, and *if* South Africa were able to avoid transferring the full principal value of those investments abroad, *then* the reduced flow of dividends and profits to foreigners would more than offset the loss of new capital inflow from abroad. South Africa would be better off in financial terms if it could completely stop doing business with foreign private investors. In the 1980s, the combination of macroeconomic policies and the introduction of the financial rand has effectively accomplished this objective for a large fraction of foreign investment, particularly for U.S. companies.

The above points are related to an important macroeconomic question. What has been, and what might be, the effect of foreign capital inflow on economic development in South Africa? A variety of estimates have been made to answer this question, but a great deal depends on the assumptions underlying the exercise. The standard assumption relative to South Africa is that dividends and profits from past investments will continue to flow abroad, and that a reduction in the inflow of foreign capital will reduce financing for investment in the domestic economy. With reduced investment, economic growth will decline and employment opportunities will diminish. While this is plausible, it is by no means the *only* plausible assumption. The productivity of new capital investment in South Africa has fallen substantially since the late 1960s, despite the improvement in the country's international terms of trade including gold. Much of the rate of future growth depends on changes in the productivity, not the level, of investment. Further, domestic saving replaced the large inflows of foreign capital in the immediate post–World War II period. For the past 20–30 years South Africa has financed virtually all of its growth from domestic investment. The simple relationship between foreign investment and economic growth posited both by South African authorities and by critics of the government has not been true in the past, nor is it likely to be true in the future. Reforms in other aspects of domestic economic policy could substantially change the potential effects of reduced, or increased, flows of foreign investment on domestic output. In particular, the steady decline in the productivity of investment since the late 1960s, shown dramatically in chapter 6, is substantially greater than the changes either in domestic investment or in foreign investment over the postwar years.

The question arises about the relationship between foreign investment and access to technology. The assumption is often made that foreign direct investment brings with it technology as well as capital—that is, it has qualitative as well as quantitative effects—and that a cessation of foreign direct investment would deprive South Africa of its access to technology. Experience both in South Africa and elsewhere makes it clear that the assumption about access is not valid. The most dramatic example is the dominant position of the Japanese in the automotive sector of South African manufacturing. Japanese firms have no direct investment in South Africa; rather, Japan achieves dominance, and technology transfer, entirely on a product and technology-licensing basis. The South African armaments industry is also based on licensing of technology rather than direct investment. The Japanese economy itself, of course, is the world's leading example of extensive use of foreign technology without substantial foreign direct investment. A reduction in foreign direct investment in South Africa would not reduce the access of the South African economy to advanced technology unless accompanied by a variety of additional measures that prohibited technology transfer.

Finally, short-term credits to the South African economy grew substantially beginning in the mid-1970s. As a trading economy with relatively high shares of imports and exports as a percentage of GDP, South Africa makes extensive use of trade credits, usually of less than a year's duration and often of 60–90 days. As an economy subject to international fluctuations, it is in need of both international currency reserves and access to short-term capital to offset variations in foreign receipts and expenditures. I know of no good estimate of the volume of trade credit South Africa has enjoyed in the past. However, the government's refusal in 1985 to pay principal on short-term loans had an immediate effect on the access of South African banks and traders to short-term bank credit other than trade credits. Debt service continued on the trade credits outside the standstill net. In the absence of short-term credit, the economy had to rebuild its own foreign reserve position so that it could meet fluctuations as well as repay loans on a basis that would keep the commercial banks reasonably happy. However, once the buildup in reserves was made, the South African economy had no further burden other than to provide enough trade finance to *increase* its total foreign transactions and continue servicing loans. By 1987 South Africa had accumulated substantial foreign reserves with which to finance its short-term credit needs and buffer changes in export earnings or import payments, and it seemed to have returned to a relatively good standing with international credit institutions.

GEOGRAPHIC DISTRIBUTION OF TRADE AND INVESTMENT

Table 3.4 gives some indication of the relative importance of different countries and areas of the world trading with and investing in South Africa. Because of statistical limitations, the figures on the regional composition of trade do not present a full picture for South Africa. The government reports South African trade on behalf of the entire Southern African Customs Union region (Botswana, Lesotho, Namibia, South Africa, and Swaziland). Therefore, the figures reported for South African exports include, for example, diamond exports from Botswana and Namibia, which together are substantially larger than those from South Africa itself. Likewise, the export figures *exclude* South Africa's exports to the other countries in the Customs Union and

TABLE 3.4. DIRECTION OF SOUTH AFRICAN TRADE, 1982–1987

Country	1982	1985	1986	1987
	Suppliers of South African Imports % of World Total			
USA	19.9	16.0	14.2	12.7
UK	17.5	17.2	15.3	15.5
FRG	21.3	22.4	23.7	25.3
France	5.4	5.1	5.0	4.6
Japan	13.8	13.6	16.7	18.7
Total	*74.5*	*74.3*	*74.9*	*76.8*
	Markets for South African Exports % of World Total			
USA	18.5	19.8	20.3	12.7
UK	11.9	11.4	10.0	9.8
FRG	11.5	9.8	11.3	11.4
France	6.7	5.8	4.0	5.3
Japan	16.9	17.0	18.5	22.3
Total	*65.5*	*63.8*	*64.1*	*61.5*

Source: U.S. General Accounting Office, Report to Congress, *South African Trends in Trade, Lending, and Investments,* September 1988.

therefore substantially understate the importance of manufactured exports, as well as the importance of African markets for South Africa's exports. The flow of investment, which is dominated by investment from Great Britain, shows a considerably higher degree of country concentration than does the flow of trade. Indeed, South Africa has a relatively dispersed trading pattern both for imports and for exports, and the dispersion has increased over time. The countries of the Organization for Economic Cooperation and Development are clearly of major importance both as sources of imports and as destinations for exports. Some of the shifts in trading patterns are due to changes in marketing arrangements; for instance, rough diamonds now go largely to Switzerland, whereas for decades they went to Great Britain. In recent years some of the changes have been a response to trade sanctions.

One principal conclusion from looking at the regional and country distribution of South Africa's trade is that actions by any single country could have only limited effect on South Africa, even if those actions were completely effective in eliminating trading or investment relationships for the country in question.

A coordinated effort of several countries would be required to affect a majority of imports or exports.

PEOPLE

The last major area of interaction between South Africa and the world economy is through the flow of people: immigration and emigration. The substantial movement of black workers between other areas in southern Africa and South Africa—over 300,000 for registered jobs at any one time and well over 1 million when seasonal and illegal migrants are counted—is not even recorded in the country's official migration statistics. The importance of white immigration and emigration is worth repeating. Gross and net flows of immigration have fluctuated considerably as political and economic conditions have changed both in the world economy and in South Africa. The Nationalist government initially adopted a policy toward immigration that differed from its predecessors, partly because of the historical Afrikaner antagonism toward *Uitlanders* (foreigners) in general and toward English-speaking immigrants in particular. From 1949 to 1962 net immigration was less than 4,000 per year. Nonetheless, there has been net immigration into South Africa throughout the postwar period; total immigration from 1947 to 1987 exceeded 1 million, and net immigration exceeded 600,000. The total white population in 1986 was just under 5 million.

A major question that has been raised for the last decade or more is whether South Africa's racial policies and their effect on political stability and economic prosperity will cause white South Africans to emigrate. In view of the present importance of the white population in providing the bulk of high-level skilled and technical manpower, the economic effect of any substantial white emigration would be disproportionate to the total numbers, particularly if such emigration took place from key sectors of the economy.

GOVERNMENT POLICIES

The South African government has long been aware of its openness to international trade and investment. A nationalistic response of import substitution began in the 1920s, and domestically managed mining finance houses were developed well before World War II. Additional policies have been adopted over the past fifteen to twenty years to deal with the possibility that increased international pressure might deny South Africa its historical trade and investment opportunities.

These policies fall into three categories. First, South Africa has made substantial investments in strategic industries. The Armaments Corporation of South Africa (ARMSCOR) was established in response to the original voluntary arms boycott. South Africa has acquired advanced technologies in arms production through a variety of licensing arrangements and is now an exporter of several classes of weapons. The most visible of the strategic industries, perhaps, are the coal gasification operations. SASOL is estimated to produce one-third of total liquid fuel requirements, using the country's extensive coal reserves. Beyond these dramatic examples, the pattern of import substitution in a range of industries reflects the desire of the South African authorities to become independent of international suppliers for a wide variety of higher-technology goods.

Second, South Africa has developed a range of expertise and institutions for sanctions busting. I know of no solid or systematic information on this activity, but both the private and the public sectors have been active in establishing companies throughout the world that could be used for transshipment and relabeling of imports and exports, as well as for changing the nationality of asset ownership in the face of increased trade and investment sanctions. Official South African statements carry a clear message about preparations.

Finally, South Africa has dealt with growing international pressures by instituting some significant changes in its overall macroeconomic management policies. Beginning in 1979, South Africa dropped its practice of pegging the rand to a major international currency, and adopted a much more active exchange rate management policy without publicly stating how the rate would be set. This action was a response to increased international uncertainty, as well as the falling gold price, in the period after 1981 when the authorities allowed the rand to drop substantially in value. The South African economy has been relatively flat in macroeconomic terms for the decade of the 1980s. But the active use of exchange rate policy encouraged new export production, maintained profitability in minerals when international prices were low, and stimulated import substitution over a wide range of commodities. All these factors permitted a more orderly response in the domestic economy than would have been possible under a fixed rate system, or under one that led to sudden and large devaluations in response to macroeconomic crises.

In addition, South Africa has used exchange controls and a dual exchange rate system, known as the financial rand, to deal with uncertainties in capital movements and to isolate the effect of capital flight from the foreign exchange reserves. The financial rand is a successor to blocked rand accounts initially introduced in the 1960s in response to the capital flight after Sharpeville. An informal market in blocked rand was converted to a securities rand in 1976, but it was abolished in early 1983 as part of an exchange rate unification, following a major review of monetary policies and institutions. The government introduced the financial rand in 1985 as a response to the credit and debt crisis. Under this mechanism, equity investors who wish to take funds out of South Africa buy the foreign currency not at the commercial banks' rate, but at a rate determined by the supply and demand for foreign exchange for capital movement purposes only. If more capital is flowing out of than into South Africa in a given period of time, the value of the financial rand will fall, and the price of foreign currency will rise. As a result of this mechanism, individuals or firms wishing to disinvest from South Africa are able to take out of the country only as much foreign currency as other foreigners wish to bring in during the same period. The introduction of the financial rand has had a major impact on the potential leverage that foreign investors exert on South Africa. It should be noted that the figures given earlier on the value of foreign investment in South Africa were converted from rand to dollars using the ordinary, or commercial, rate of exchange. If the financial rand had been used, the figures for the present value of foreign assets in South Africa would have been substantially lower. By the end of 1985 the financial rand was worth only 70 percent of the commercial rand, and at the end of 1986 it was worth less than half. It has generally fluctuated around a 25–40 percent discount from the commercial rand.

The attitude of the South African authorities toward foreign investment is an interesting one and has to do more with psychology than with economics, as the following observations illustrate.

- The figures cited above make it clear that flows of foreign investment have not been of substantial importance to South Africa in quantitative terms for more than 30 years; yet the authorities have continued to attribute a much greater importance to them than the facts support.

- Repatriated dividends and profits have long been well in excess of the flows of new investment, including reinvestment. Furthermore, the financial rand mechanism has made it possible for South Africa to expropriate much of the value of foreign investment if an investor decides to move out of the country. The government simply refuses to make foreign exchange available from general sources, and the investor takes what can be found in the financial rand market. Yet the government has mounted a major campaign against disinvestment by foreign equity investors.

- Exchange control regulations permit investment to come in via the financial rand, but stipulate that dividends and profits can be repatriated through the commercial rand. In other words, a foreign investor buys rand cheap and sells rand dear. The private investor profits nicely, but the country could easily lose.[5] The authorities encourage foreign investment of this sort, even though analysts of such practices in any other country would point out how the rules allow the investor to benefit at the expense of the country. In short, the attention paid to the role of foreign investment in South Africa seems well out of proportion to its recent economic importance.

Several conclusions can be drawn from the attitudes of the South African government and foreign investors. First, the two are allies in the antisanctions campaign in the industrialized countries. Second, the link between direct investment and access to technology is an easy one, even if it is not the only way to acquire know-how. Third, foreign investment has been put to very specific uses at various times since 1970, such as the financing of key parastatals and for balance-of-payments support during weak commodity markets, even though the overall importance of foreign capital to South Africa has been traditionally low. Finally, after the buildup of short-term debt in the 1980s and the standstill on principal repayments in 1985, the authorities have tried to meet the obligation for principal repayments. In the absence of rollovers of loans (which would keep total foreign liabilities constant), South Africa has had to export capital. Having made the adjustment to no gross or net inflows in 1985–1987, the authorities would clearly prefer to avoid continued outflows through repayment without rollovers.

The overall relationship between South Africa and the world, and the country's vulnerability to changes in world conditions or opinion, may be summed up as follows: South Africa still has a relatively high degree of concentration in and dependence on mineral exports. But the majority of its minerals are high-value, low-bulk commodities that have a major share in world trade, or are anonymous in character, or both. Unlike comparable countries, South Africa has not yet become a major exporter of a wide range of manufactured goods, except to regional markets. Trade is quite dispersed by country and geographic region for both imports and exports, and South Africa's vulnerability to action by a single country is therefore considerably diminished. Substantial international cooperation would be needed in order to have a major effect on South Africa. The country's principal trading vulnerability still would seem to be in its dependence on oil imports, though its high-bulk coal exports are difficult to hide and therefore relatively likely to be hit by sanctions. Foreign investment provided an important share of the financing of total capital formation in South Africa for many decades, but has not done so for the past thirty years. Further, the flow of foreign direct investment for many years has involved mainly the reinvestment of dividends and profits earned from South Africa itself, and the outward flow of dividends and profits has long exceeded the flow of new investment. Overall, dependence on foreign investment is a good deal less than one would conclude from the vehemence of the discussion surrounding it. Finally, the South African authorities have taken a variety of steps aimed at reducing the vulnerability of the economy to changes in the international situation, by providing investments in import-replacement industries, preparing for trade sanctions through a variety of alternative trading arrangements, and adopting macroeconomic policies, including the financial rand, to cushion or isolate the effects of international events.

4

SOUTH AFRICA AND THE REGION

South Africa is a small country in the world economy. In regional terms, however, it has always been been a powerful economic force. The imperial dreams of Cecil Rhodes are still reflected in many of the significant economic relationships within the region. Major investments by South African mining houses, particularly the Anglo-American DeBeers group, go back half a century in former Northern and Southern Rhodesia (now Zambia and Zimbabwe). South Africa had important trade and transport links with Mozambique when the latter was a Portuguese colony. For decades DeBeers was active in Angola and Tanzania in the mining and marketing of diamonds, and it is the only foreign entity involved in Botswana's diamond production and marketing today. Since the late nineteenth century, the gold mining companies extended their reach throughout southern Africa in the recruitment of black labor for South Africa's mines. Earlier in the nineteenth century Britain annexed the port of Natal to curb Afrikaner economic power. Rhodes, as prime minister of the Cape, and Transvaal President Paul Kruger both recognized the strategic significance of the region's transportation network and struggled to achieve control. Many parallels exist between these events and the tensions between South Africa and its neighbors in modern times. South Africa is of fundamental economic importance to the rest of southern Africa. Conversely, the region is of great importance to South Africa, strategically, economically, and financially.

ECONOMIC RELATIONS IN SOUTHERN AFRICA

In 1980, the nine independent countries of the region—Angola, Botswana, Lesotho, Malawi, Mozambique, Swaziland, Tanzania,

Zambia, and Zimbabwe—established the Southern African Development Coordination Conference (SADCC). A primary objective of the new organization was to increase its members' independence from the regional dominance of South Africa, principally by reorganizing and reconstructing the transportation system. That system, destroyed by the wars of independence in Angola and Mozambique, was kept inoperative by continued armed conflicts, supported and financed in part by South Africa. SADCC has become an important regional organization and has performed a major role in coordinating donor assistance to regional projects, particularly in transportation and communication.

South Africa is clearly the economically dominant country in the region, contributing about three-quarters of regional GDP and two-thirds of exports (see Table 4.1).[1] It should be stressed, however, that South Africa has less than a third of the region's total population of 100 million people. Because of its extensive economic relationships with the region, as well as its activities in supporting guerrilla organizations in several countries and taking military action in virtually every country there, South Africa's policies have an important impact on a region much larger than itself. The South African government has for decades defined its internal problems in regional terms, and its policies reflect the view that the region is important in dealing with domestic problems.

Some of the interdependence within the region is indicated in the data in Table 4.2 and Table 4.3. South Africa is a major trading partner for seven of the SADCC countries, a fact that the South African authorities like to stress (as, for instance, in their public relations brochure *South Africa: Mainstay of Southern Africa*). In 1984 South Africa was a market for 13 percent of the exports and supplied 49 percent of the imports of the six landlocked SADCC states. What is also obvious from the tables, however, is the importance of South Africa's own exports to the SADCC countries, as well as the net balance-of-payments surplus South Africa has with SADCC. South Africa's $1.3 billion visible trade surplus with SADCC in 1984 was the equivalent of over 40 percent of its overall current account surplus. By 1988 and 1989

TABLE 4.1. BASIC DATA: SOUTHERN AFRICA, 1984

Country	Area (000 km²)	Population (millions)	GDP (billions of U.S. $)	Exports (billions of U.S. $)	Imports (billions of U.S. $)	GDP per capita (U.S. $)
Angola	1,247	9.9	4.7	2.10	1.10	470
Botswana	600	1.0	1.0	0.67	0.55	990
Lesotho	30	1.5	0.4	0.02	0.43	240
Malawi	118	6.8	1.1	0.31	0.27	160
Mozambique	802	13.4	2.8	0.18	0.55	210
Swaziland	17	0.7	0.6	0.27	0.35	770
Tanzania	45	21.5	4.4	0.38	0.85	200
Zambia	753	6.4	2.6	0.68	0.61	410
Zimbabwe	391	8.1	4.6	1.16	0.95	570
SADCC	*4,903*	*69.3*	*22.2*	*5.77*	*5.66*	*320*
Namibia	824	1.1	1.2	0.75	0.76	1,100
All ten	*5,727*	*70.4*	*23.4*	*6.52*	*6.42*	*330*
South Africa	1,221	31.6	73.4	18.03	15.04	2,320
Southern Africa	*6,948*	*102.0*	*96.8*	*24.55*	*21.46*	*950*

Sources: Most data are from World Bank, *World Development Report, 1986* (Washington, D.C., 1986). The following exceptions apply: GDP figures for Mozambique are estimates based on World Bank, *World Tables,* 3rd ed. (Washington, D.C., 1974), and information from Economist Intelligence Unit (EIU) reports and other sources. GDP and trade figures for Namibia are based on various Namibian sources cited in EIU reports and elsewhere. Trade data for other countries come from International Monetary Fund (IMF), *Director of Trade Statistics Year-book, 1986* (Washington, D.C., 1986), or from IMF, *International Financial Statistics,* recent issues. Both sources report imports and exports on an FOB basis.

Note: The South African trade statistics have been adjusted from the published data, since the IMF and World Bank give South Africa's own data, which include the entire Southern Africa Customs Union and cover only trade between the Union as a whole and the rest of the world. On the basis of trade data for Namibia, Botswana, Lesotho, and Swaziland, their trade with the rest of the world was eliminated from the published South Africa data; their trade with South Africa was retained. As a result, reported South African exports of $17.38 billion have been adjusted to $18.03 billion, and reported imports of $14.97 billion have been adjusted to $15.04 billion.

that surplus was probably larger still. The importance of regional trade for South Africa is even greater if Namibia is included in the calculation.

South Africa has consistently run a balance-of-trade surplus with the countries of the region, as the data in Table 4.3 illustrate. During periods of relative foreign exchange scarcity and balance-of-payments difficulties (South Africa faced both from the mid-1970s to the late 1980s), the large trade surpluses with the region have been of special significance to the South African

TABLE 4.2.   INTRAREGIONAL SOUTHERN AFRICAN TRADE, 1984
(MILLIONS OF U.S. $)

Country	Exports			Imports			Trade balance		
	Total	To SADCC	To South Africa	Total	From SADCC	From South Africa	Total	With SADCC	With South Africa
Angola	2,061	0	0	1,018	2	0	1,043	-2	0
Botswana	674	27	59	706	62	552	-32	-36	-493
Lesotho	24	0	8	498	1	370	-474	-1	-362
Malawi	314	27	23	270	30	109	44	-3	-86
Mozambique	180	21	8	549	28	64	-369	-7	-56
Swaziland	270	4	100	350	1	315	-80	3	215
Tanzania	377	7	0	847	9	0	-470	-2	0
Zambia	678	28	5	608	45	129	70	-17	-124
Zimbabwe	1,156	131	212	955	67	184	201	64	28
SADCC	5,734	245	415	5,801	245	1,723	-67	0	-1,308
Namibia	753	0	188	761	0	685	-8	0	-497
All ten	6,487	245	603	6,562	245	2,408	-75	0	-1,805
South Africa	18,030	1,723	0	15,042	415	2,408	2,988	1,308	0

Sources: Based on IMF, *Direction of Trade Statistics Yearbook, 1986* (Washington, D.C., 1986), with the following exceptions: Botswana, Lesotho, and Swaziland, as well as Namibia (collectively, NBLS), are not included in the IMF data, as South Africa reports for the whole of the Customs Union. Therefore, the South African figures were adjusted by subtracting NBLS exports to and imports from countries outside the Union, and then adding NBLS exports to and imports from South Africa. Trade data for Botswana, Lesotho, and Swaziland were taken from country statistical publications, supplemented by data from EIU publications. The Namibian data are from official publications as reported by the EIU. Botswana trade with Zimbabwe is based on Botswana data rather than IMF data, since I believe the former are more accurate. The IMF reports both imports and exports on an FOB basis; Botswana, Lesotho, and Swaziland report imports on a CIF basis and exports on an FOB basis.

TABLE 4.3. BALANCE OF TRADE: SADCC COUNTRIES AND
SOUTH AFRICA, 1970–1984
(*MILLIONS OF CURRENT U.S. $*)

Country	With SADCC countries				With South Africa			
	1970	1979	1982	1984	1970	1979	1982	1984
Angola	1	−26	−7	−2	−8	−95	—*	—
Botswana	−3	8	16	−36	−31	−426	−542	−493
Lesotho	—	—	−1	−1	−13	−426	−488	−362
Malawi	−18	−7	−1	−3	−9	−155	−90	−86
Mozambique	1	−14	−19	−7	−29	−76	−80	−56
Swaziland	3	1	5	3	−38	−344	−317	−215
Tanzania	16	26	−6	−2	0	0	0	0
Zambia	−47	3	−13	−17	−63	−76	−140	−124
Zimbabwe	47	7	27	64	−60	−160	−147	28
SADCC	*0*	*0*	*0*	*0*	*−251*	*−1,757*	*−1,808*	*−1,308*

Sources: For 1970, G. Sollie, "Trade Patterns and Institutional Aspects of Trade: An
Empirical Study of Trade in Southern Africa," *DERAP Working Paper,* no. A267,
1982. For 1979 and 1982, United Nations Industrial Development Organization
(UNIDO), *Industrial Co-operation through the Southern African Development Coor-
dination Conference* (Vienna, 1985). For 1984, see IMF, *Direction of Trade Statistics
Yearbook,* 1986 (Washington, D.C., 1986).

* — = less than 0.5 million.

economy. The importance of the capacity to pay for imports
suggests that the multiplier effect on domestic output may be at
least three to four times the value of export earnings, a figure
supported by offical South African sources.

Disaggregating South African–SADCC trade reveals a
number of additional points of interest. South Africa is the only
supplier of petroleum products to Botswana, Lesotho, and
Swaziland (the BLS states), and from time to time has been a
critical supplier to Malawi and Zimbabwe. It supplies virtually all
electricity in Lesotho, Swaziland, and much of southern Mozambique.[2] South Africa in most years has provided substantial food
to deficit countries in the region, although Zimbabwe's recent
surpluses could prove to be an effective substitute. The impact of
South African–backed guerrillas in *disrupting* food production
and transportation in Angola and Mozambique also should be
noted. SADCC markets are a substantial outlet for some South
African manufacturing industries, accounting for 40 percent or
more of exports. In addition, McFarland showed that exports to
Botswana, Lesotho, and Swaziland alone accounted for nearly a

quarter of the total growth of South Africa's manufacturing sector during the 1970s.[3] Given the continued growth of the BLS economies in the last few years and the economic stagnation in South Africa, the importance of regional exports to South African manufacturing growth must be even greater today.

Perhaps the most critical variable in explaining interdependence within the region is its transportation system. Map 4.1 shows the regional rail network and ports in both the SADCC countries and South Africa. By 1987 the vast majority of trade of the landlocked SADCC states was being carried through the ports of South Africa, not through the SADCC ports in Angola, Mozambique, and Tanzania. While some SADCC traffic has always flowed through the South African Transport System (SATS), the volume has increased substantially over the last twenty years. The major reasons are that the Benguela railway to Lobito in Angola was cut by the South African–backed UNITA guerrillas; the railways to Nacala and Maputo in Mozambique at times were completely disrupted by the dissident MNR forces, also supported by South Africa; and the route to Beira frequently has been limited to a small number of trains per day by the same guerrilla forces. The Tazara railway from Zambia to Dar es Salaam has never operated at full capacity, and even if it were to do so, it would handle only a fraction of the total SADCC trade. For all the SADCC countries, except Zambia, the route through Dar es Salaam would be substantially longer in both time and distance than the other SADCC outlets or the routes through South Africa. The struggle for control and manipulation of the regional transport routes that preoccupied Paul Kruger and Cecil Rhodes in the late nineteenth century continues in southern Africa today.

Until the regional transportation system is reconstructed to give the SADCC countries secure and dependable alternative routes independent of South Africa, these countries will have difficulty finding trading partners other than South Africa, even where the economics make sense. It should be noted that with the decline in the value of the rand during the 1980s, the competitive position of South African products in SADCC markets has improved substantially.

Another major category of interdependence in southern

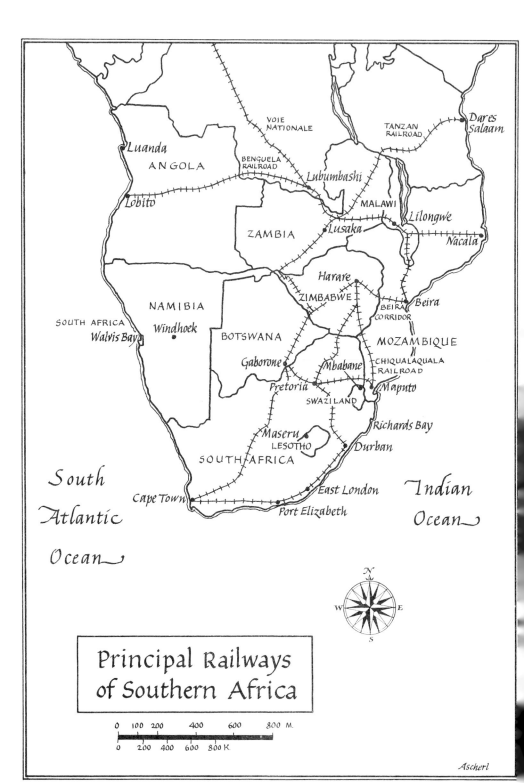

Principal Railways
of Southern Africa

Africa is the flow of migrant labor from the region to work in South Africa, principally in the mines but also in other sectors. While the exact number of black workers from the SADCC states employed in South Africa is difficult to establish, several points are clear. First, the total flow of black labor is substantial and important to the economies of the SADCC countries and South Africa. In recent years approximately 350,000 SADCC citizens have had recorded contract employment in South Africa; these workers comprise about half of the black labor force in the mines. Perhaps another million workers from SADCC states are employed in South Africa either illegally or seasonally.

Second, the employment of black workers from SADCC countries has been important since the beginning of the gold mining industry in South Africa (see Table 4.4). Only since the mid-1980s have non–South African sources provided less than half of the total black labor in the gold mines, and they generally have provided three-fifths or more.

Third, the trend of regional recruitment is downward. Starting in the mid-1970s, after the large increases in the real wage of black mine workers, as well as other changes in the gold mining industry and in South Africa generally, the recruitment of mine workers changed in two respects. Growing emphasis was placed on recruitment from within South Africa, in part because of the recognition that an increasingly explosive political situation was inherent in widespread African unemployment. The number of black mine workers from all sources who were offered new contracts also declined substantially. While the practice for

TABLE 4.4.   EMPLOYMENT OF SADCC CITIZENS
IN SOUTH AFRICAN GOLD MINES

Measure	1896–1898	1906	1926	1946	1966	1975	1985
Number (000)	35	62	119	179	253	220	195
As % of black workers	64.6	77.1	58.7	58.7	66.0	68.4	43.2

Sources: For 1896–1966, Francis Wilson, *Labour in the South African Gold Mines 1911–1969* (London: Cambridge University Press, 1972). For 1975 and 1985, Chamber of Mines of South Africa, *Ninety-fifth Annual Report 1984* (Johannesburg, 1985).

many decades had been to recruit very young blacks for mining jobs and to accept a substantial turnover, the mines consciously aimed at reducing labor turnover and increasing the experience of existing workers. As a result, the 350,000 legal foreign workers in South Africa are, on the average, a much more experienced group than were their counterparts a decade or two ago. Consequently, they are considerably more valuable to the South African economy.

The migrant labor system entails numerous economic, social, and political difficulties for the SADCC states. While these countries as a group struggle to increase employment opportunities at home, the system provides employment, cash income, and an important source of foreign exchange earnings. Most SADCC governments have arrangements that provide for the compulsory remittance of a portion of mine workers' pay through the South African authorities and their own central banks in order to ensure they receive the foreign exchange earned by their miners in South Africa.

South Africa has a variety of other connections with its neighbors. The country's investment is present in most of the SADCC countries. It is dominated by the mining investments of the Anglo-American DeBeers group, but is sizable in manufacturing, finance, trade, and other sectors as well. A large number of South African citizens working in the SADCC countries are related to that investment. While their numbers are much smaller than those of blacks from SADCC states working in South Africa, their average earnings are considerably higher. South Africa also earns substantial revenue from trade in services with the SADCC countries. Insurance, finance, freight forwarding and clearing, repair services, and a variety of other activities link South Africa with most of the SADCC members.

Table 4.5 provides a summary estimate for recent years of the overall balance-of-payments effect of trade, investment, and movements of labor between SADCC countries and South Africa. In most cases, the net payments flow from the SADCC states to South Africa. The only significant exceptions are the labor remittances and pensions flowing in the other direction, and the payments to Botswana, Lesotho, and Swaziland under the Cus-

TABLE 4.5. SOUTH AFRICA'S NET CURRENT ACCOUNT SURPLUS
WITH SADCC COUNTRIES, MID-1980s
(MILLIONS OF U.S. $)

Measure	*Net receipts*	*Net payments*
Visible trade	1,300–1,500	
Invisibles		
Transport	200–300	
Other nonfactor services	100–200	
Labor remittances, pensions, etc.		
From South Africa		200–350
From SADCC	50–100	
Profits and dividends	100–150	
Customs Union*		300
Total	1,750–2,250	500–650
Overall balance	*1,250–1,600*	

Source: Steven Lewis, "Some Economic Realities in Southern Africa: One Hundred
Million Futures," in Coralie Bryant, ed., *Poverty, Policy, and Food Security in Southern Africa* (Boulder: Lynne Rienner Publishers, Inc., 1988).

* These represent gross payments from the Customs Union pool. Taxes paid by the BLS
to the pool are partially included in the CIF value of these countries' imports from
South Africa. Payments into the pool for excise duties paid on excisable production in
the BLS and for import duties or surcharges on goods imported from outside the
Union by the BLS are not available, but represent flows to South Africa from the BLS.

toms Union agreements. In aggregate, the net balance-of-payments deficit of the SADCC countries with South Africa ranges between $1.2 billion and $1.6 billion. Since South Africa extends little credit to the region, the vast majority of this deficit is settled in hard currencies. Therefore, in addition to the effect on employment and aggregate demand in South Africa, there is a substantial benefit in foreign exchange. Government estimates suggest that the multiplier effect of increased net export earnings on growth of income and production in South Africa is at least one and one-half times as large as any increase in domestic demand would be, since increased exports relax the foreign exchange constraint the country faces.

The concept of the SADCC's "dependence" on South Africa is promoted strongly by South African government sources and is accepted by both SADCC countries and most international analysts. It is, however, somewhat misleading. While South Africa is undoubtedly a dominant partner in many respects, it benefits substantially from its economic relationships with the SADCC states. "Interdependence," albeit asymmetric, is a much better way to describe the relationships among the countries in the region.

INSTITUTIONAL ARRANGEMENTS

In addition to the quantifiable economic relationships between South Africa and the SADCC countries, a variety of important institutional arrangements in the region should be considered. Some involve South Africa with SADCC countries, and others exclude South Africa. Finally, mention should be made of the South African government's own vision of a "constellation of states in southern Africa."

In the agreements establishing the Union of South Africa, provision was made for the Customs Union, to include the High Commission Territories of Bechuanaland, Basutoland, and Swaziland. The arrangements provided that a fixed share of the total pool of customs and excise revenue collected within the common customs area would be paid to these three territories. Following the independence of Botswana, Lesotho, and Swaziland, their governments undertook a renegotiation of the terms of the Customs Union and reached a new agreement, which was signed in 1969. This agreement retained the common external tariff and common excise duties in all four countries and left the setting of tariffs and tax rates to the government of South Africa. Certain provisions allow the individual countries to undertake measures of protection against imports from each other, but these have seldom been invoked. The Customs Union is the principal reason why the BLS countries are more closely integrated with the South African economy than are the other SADCC countries.

The revenue arrangements of the Customs Union are important to the BLS, especially to Lesotho and Swaziland, since they provide for revenue to be paid to the BLS on the basis of the total value of their imports from all sources worldwide. In 1976 payments were set at a minimum of 17 percent and a maximum of 23 percent of the value of imports, regardless of the level of duties collected in the common customs pool. In most years the percentage has been near the floor of the range. As the BLS economies grew rapidly in the 1960s and 1970s, this arrangement offered a rapidly increasing source of government revenue. As indicated in Table 4.5, the gross payments from South Africa to the BLS in recent years have been about $300 million annually. However, this revenue is substantially offset by several factors, including the higher prices of South African–made goods paid for by the BLS because of the protective tariff, payments into the customs pool of excise duties within the BLS, and customs duties collected on imports from outside the common customs area and paid into the pool by the BLS. The formula also provides for revenue payment two years in arrears. Therefore, any higher tariffs or excises are payable immediately by BLS importers, but increased revenue to the BLS governments is paid two years later.

The details of the revenue-sharing arrangements have been a matter of debate between the BLS and South Africa for a number of years. According to press reports, the three smaller countries feel that the arrangements insufficiently compensate them for the disadvantages of belonging to the Customs Union with a more highly industrialized partner, especially the subsidy inherent in paying protected prices to South African manufacturers. South Africa, on the other hand, has expressed concern about the rising cost involved in the payments from the Customs Union. While the BLS share of the customs revenue pool was 3–4 percent after the 1969 renegotiation, by 1984–1985 it had risen to 14 percent, which reflected in large part that the BLS economies grew more rapidly than South Africa's.[4]

An important part of South Africa's concern about budgetary costs, however, is the fact that when Transkei, Bophuthatswana, Venda, and Ciskei were declared "independent," the South African government agreed to provide them with the same revenue-sharing arrangements as the BLS had through the Customs Union. Consequently, by 1984–1985 the South African government was paying a total of 35 percent of its gross customs and excise revenue to the BLS and the "independent" homelands (14 percent and 21 percent, respectively). The decision to extend Customs Union arrangements to these four homelands would appear to be one of many decisions regarding the development of the homelands that the South African government failed to think through. Since Customs Union revenue is paid directly to the homeland governments, South Africa has little control over how it is used. Pretoria apparently has concerns, however, about how the revenue, which amounts to several hundred million dollars annually, is being spent.

Lesotho and Swaziland are part of the Rand Monetary Area with South Africa. Although the two smaller countries have established their own currencies, the rand continues to circulate in both, and the local currencies trade at par with South African currency. South Africa generally holds the foreign exchange reserves on behalf of all three countries, and it makes payments to Lesotho and Swaziland to reflect this fact.

Several other agreements involve South Africa with one or more of the SADCC states. A bilateral trade agreement between Zimbabwe and South Africa provides for a range of tariff preferences between them. This arrangement predated Zimbabwe's independence and has been continued, with modifications, ever since. South Africa also has an agreement with Mozambique regarding the supply of power generated at the Cabora Bassa hydroelectric project (built during the Portuguese colonial era) to the South African grid. Constant sabotage has virtually eliminated the flow of electricity from Cabora Bassa and, consequently, has caused losses for both countries. In 1988 South Africa, Mozambique, and Portugal reached agreement on a plan to secure the power lines and restore the flow of electricity. A major scheme just getting underway is the Highlands Water Project in Lesotho, which is intended to provide hydroelectric power and water for South Africa through a series of dams in Lesotho.

Three multilateral and one bilateral arrangement not involving South Africa should be noted. During the war for independence of Zimbabwe, an informal grouping of Angola, Botswana, Mozambique, Tanzania, and Zambia—known as the Front Line States (FLS)—was formed. The group, which now includes Zimbabwe, has no permanent secretariat and meets on an ad hoc basis to consider issues related to the political and security relationships between South Africa and its neighbors.

SADCC—which grew out of the Front Line States and includes all its members plus Lesotho, Malawi, and Swaziland—is committed to increasing the independence of its nine member countries from South Africa's economic domination. It has a small secretariat and operates on "functionalist" principles, setting achievable targets of cooperation, in the spheres of transportation and communication, as well as food security and agricultural research. The degree of cooperation among countries and the common approach to the international lending agencies that SADCC has fostered are unique in the developing world. SADCC has stayed away from commitments to broad economic integration among the countries or expanded multilateral trade, though it has facilitated a number of bilateral trading deals.

The Preferential Trade Area for Eastern and Southern Africa (PTA) includes most of the SADCC countries plus a number of states farther north and east. The PTA, unlike SADCC, has an elaborate treaty and protocols, which specify objectives in terms of free multilateral trade, reduction of tariff barriers among member countries, and arrangements for multilateral clearing of payments among countries. It includes a variety of "rules of origin," defining what goods will be subject to tariff preferences among the countries. It also discriminates against goods produced in PTA countries by companies in which non-PTA citizens own the majority of shares. Both Kenya and Zimbabwe have some difficulty under these arrangements, and specific transitional provisions were made for Zimbabwe in recognition of its relatively late independence. In addition, the protocols call for discrimination against South Africa, although they provide a special arrangement for the BLS because of these countries' unusual relationship with South Africa. The PTA has moved somewhat slowly, since virtually all member countries have extensive exchange and import control systems. Tariff preferences are, in many respects, a minor issue in determining the direction of trade for the group's members.

An important bilateral arrangement is the Botswana-Zimbabwe trade agreement, which originated in the colonial period and provides for tariff-free trade. Since Botswana is in the Customs Union with South Africa, an interesting result is that exports from Zimbabwe to Botswana enjoy protection from the South African tariff.[5]

Finally, there is South Africa's own vision of regional development, which has its origins deep in South African history. As a part of its grand design for the region, the South African government developed in the 1970s the notion of a "constellation of states in southern Africa." The initial idea was that this would include not only the South African homelands but also other states in the region, particularly the BLS. South Africa sees itself as the regional economic power and hub, and the constellation of states was intended to be the economic and financial vehicle for exercising that part of its regional domination. A variety of institutions were involved, including a regional development bank. The bank has been established, but other southern African countries have shown little interest in participating in the scheme. Nonetheless, the South African government's rhetoric continues to stress the idea of regional economic cooperation centered on South Africa.

SOUTH AFRICA'S IMPACT

South Africa has made it clear that it regards southern Africa as its own sphere of influence. In the 1970s, as the Portuguese colonial empire crumbled and the war for independence in Zimbabwe intensified, South Africa initiated measures to ensure its continued economic domination in the region and its ability to control the security situation. Transportation is a key to that overall control. The effect of South African military support for UNITA in Angola and for the MNR in Mozambique has been to cut SADCC's alternative transportation links and to force its member countries to use SATS. This provides additional revenue and trade for South Africa. South Africa's policies substantially limit the independence of action of the six landlocked SADCC states, as well as that of Angola and Mozambique. South

Africa also pursues interrelated and self-reinforcing military, security, transportation, financial, and trade objectives in the region.

What are the results and implications of South Africa's regional policy? South Africa is a substantial net beneficiary of the trading arrangements and the flows of labor and capital throughout southern Africa (see Table 4.5). In addition, it has imposed *very* substantial costs on the rest of the region in a number of ways. In 1985 SADCC, making its first such estimate, calculated that the total cost to its members of South African regional policy was about $2 billion per year between 1980 and 1984. More recent figures suggest that this is an underestimate. Most of these costs are due to direct war damage, related losses in GDP, and increased defense expenditures, principally, but not exclusively, in Angola and Mozambique. The figures are in the same order of magnitude as total official development assistance to all the SADCC states during that period. Between 1984 and 1988, as the civil wars intensified in Angola and Mozambique, and as a larger and larger share of the SADCC transportation was funneled through South Africa, the costs to the SADCC countries rose. In particular, the loss of output—not to mention the loss of lives—in Angola and Mozambique increased substantially. The events of 1988 and early 1989 with regard to Angola, Namibia, and even Mozambique may suggest that the South African authorities are interested in achieving lower levels of destabilization of their neighbors without giving up their desire to substantially influence events in the region, to dominate it economically, and to deny the liberation movements bases of operation in the region.

The titles of three recent studies of South Africa's impact in the region, *Destructive Engagement, Children on the Front Line,* and *Beggar Your Neighbours*, reflect a regional view of South Africa's economic impact. While South Africa continues to emphasize in its own publications and statements, the extent to which the region depends on it for trade, transportation, and employment, two points bear repeating. First, South Africa is a substantial beneficiary of the economic links in the region. Second, South

Africa has imposed enormous costs on the rest of the region through the combination of its military actions and manipulation of the regional transport system. South Africa sees its domestic problems in regional terms, and this perspective affects the lives of the 70 million people who live in the neighboring countries. It is, therefore, important to take into account the regional dimension of South Africa's policies in considering future options.

5

EXTERNAL ECONOMIC PRESSURES AND SOUTH AFRICAN REACTIONS

The extent to which economic pressures foster political change is one of the most hotly contested issues in the policy debate concerning South Africa. This chapter examines the effects of the international economic pressures that have already been used against South Africa and the probable impact of future pressures. I have chosen the term "pressures" rather than "sanctions" to describe the use of economic means to promote change. The term "pressures" encompasses a broad range of forces, many of which may not be the result of conscious decisions by national or international policymakers. In contrast, "sanctions" has a narrower definition, describing deliberate measures adopted by foreign governments or by international institutions, such as the United Nations, the Commonwealth of Nations, and the European Economic Community.

Before discussing the impact of international economic pressures on South Africa, a few points need to be made about the use of economic pressure as an instrument of foreign policy. Economic pressure has been used by all major countries in recent years to achieve foreign policy objectives. In theory, economic pressures are controlled and targeted in the same way as other foreign policy instruments.

Unfortunately, discussions of economic pressure/sanctions as a policy tool used by foreign governments to promote change in South Africa have been blurred by several factors:

- A failure to distinguish clearly the specific measures being discussed and the processes by which they are supposed to affect economic developments, influence political behavior, and hence promote political change

- Extravagant claims concerning both the successes and the failures of past attempts to use economic pressures

- A tendency on the part of both proponents and opponents of sanctions to mix and confuse arguments about the morality of sanctions with arguments concerning their efficacy

- A failure to relate arguments about economic pressure to other processes at work in South Africa and to take into account the country's economic structure and history

- A curious and inconsistent materialism that causes advocates on the extremes of the sanctions debate to argue that individuals who share their beliefs would not change their values or their behavior on the basis of economic considerations such as loss of income, but that their opponents can be forced through economic pressure to either change their minds or lose their will to resist.

I do not address directly the questions of morality. Few advocates argue for or against sanctions on purely moral grounds. Therefore, I do not discuss the pro-sanctions position that dealing with South Africa is by definition supportive of the regime and should be avoided, or the anti-sanctions view that economic pressures should be foresworn because they will inevitably impose heavier burdens on black South Africans. Most advocates on both sides of the debate have an interest in the practical effects of economic pressure on political and economic behavior. The emphasis here is on understanding the effects of past international pressures on South Africa and the potential *economic* scope for such pressures in the future.

TYPES OF PRESSURES AND THEIR EFFECTS

It is useful to divide the types of actions that have been or may eventually be taken against South Africa into two groups: those affecting trade in goods and services (including technology), and those affecting movement of capital. Pressures from the international community to date have involved both types. It is useful, as well, to consider the impact of pressures or sanctions over various time periods, since the effects may be quite different in the short and the long run. External pressures can result in immediate losses of income, production, or employment, and can also affect the prospects for economic growth. Regardless of the time frame, the effects of international actions depend to a very large extent on the measures the South African government adopts in response to, or in anticipation of, those pressures. Finally, it should be stressed that, while only the economic reactions are considered here, the *political* reactions—both of the government and of those opposed to apartheid—are of fundamental importance to the ultimate effects of economic pressures.

The short-term effects of pressures to reduce trade are generally felt through prices. Embargoes or boycotts can be avoided—at a price. Estimates of the costs of sanctions to Southern Rhodesia during the UDI period generally put the losses at 20 percent of the value of traded goods—higher prices for imports, lower prices for exports, and a consequent loss through worsened international terms of trade. Along with such price discounts and premiums, short-term unavailabilities of goods or services often result. These effects represent real losses in income for the country subject to the pressure.

In all cases these pressures have the effect of shifting both demand and supply from international to domestic markets, forcing or inducing higher levels of self-sufficiency, and simultaneously reducing the benefits from international trade. This, in turn, can produce the same kind of reaction that generalized protectionism has in many developing countries and that occurred in South Africa during World War II: an import-substitution boom in domestic manufacturing sectors. Capital and labor are shifted from export industries to import replacements, and a period of rapid economic growth can follow, with rising incomes, employment, and output. The limit on this kind of growth depends on the productivity of resources devoted to the import-replacement industries. If productivity increases rapidly, then import substitution can go on for a considerable period. If the industries remain high-cost ones, then the process runs out and growth stops when the rest of the economy can no longer increase its subsidy to the import-replacement industries. A good deal also depends on the initial conditions when economic pressures are applied. With considerable excess capacity, for example, it may be possible to increase output with low investment costs for some time; this appears to have happened in Rhodesia.

In the longer term, international pressures to reduce trade must start to slow the potential and actual rates of growth of output and employment. Denial of access to international trade will lower the potential output per unit of capital and labor. Denial of access to international technology, often embodied in new capital equipment, will reduce the productivity of new domestic investment. And the continuation of the "tax" imposed by adverse terms of trade will mean losses, year after year, of real income relative to what might have been. Despite the growth of import-replacement industries in the short run, lack of international competitiveness in cost structures must catch up sooner or later, *unless* improved technologies can be acquired or developed.

Loss of access to capital markets has somewhat different effects. Long-term capital inflows make it possible for a country to invest more than it can save—it can increase its capital stock without having to squeeze down domestic consumption. If the flow of long-term capital is restricted, a country has to either increase its domestic saving or reduce the level of investment. Further, developing countries generally experience a more rapid growth of demand for imports than of their export earnings; foreign capital inflow can facilitate more rapid growth by financing imports and easing the balance-of-payments constraint on growth of incomes. Restrictions on foreign capital inflow would tighten the balance-of-payments constraint.

Some aspects of long-term capital inflow, particularly the flow of foreign direct investment, also involve the transfer of technology. However, some countries have unbundled technology from direct investment with notable success; Japan, for example, has done so for over a century. Direct investment and technological transfer are not necessarily linked. Japan acquired advanced technologies for decades without allowing much private direct investment. Moreover, Japanese automobiles have achieved a preeminent position in the South African market without any Japanese direct investment. Other things being equal, a loss of capital inflows would tend to reduce the level of investment and—again, *if* all things were equal—slow the growth of output and employment. South Africa's experience shows that there need not be a one-for-one relationship between changes in foreign investment and changes in domestic investment.

Finally, loss of access to short-term capital markets forces a country to carry out its transactions on a cash basis and to hold enough liquid assets to meet all short-term fluctuations in its external payments. Thus, a country without access to short-term credit would have to maintain greater international currency reserves. To reach the required level, it would have to produce more than it consumed domestically for a period of time in order to generate a surplus in its international payments.

PAST TRADE PRESSURES

Among the trade-related pressures to which South Africa has been subjected, three are of particular importance: the embargo on sales of arms and ammunition; the oil embargo imposed by the Organization of Petroleum Exporting Countries (OPEC); and the range of partial trade sanctions adopted in recent years by the United States, the Commonwealth of Nations, and the European Communities. In the area of investment, two types of pressure can be distinguished. The first is disinvestment by foreign banks and corporations that have been under growing pressure to leave South Africa since the 1960s. The second is the decision of the international banks in 1985 not to roll over credits to South Africa, which resulted in the standstill on payments on much of South Africa's foreign debt.

Arms Embargo

While individual countries had undertaken earlier actions to reduce their economic dealings with South Africa, the first serious international action on trade was the UN Security Council resolution of 1963 that "called upon" countries to stop trade in arms and ammunition with South Africa: the embargo was voluntary. In 1977 the Security Council adopted mandatory restrictions. However, existing licensing arrangements with South

Africa were not subject to the compulsory embargo; UN members were again "called upon" to terminate them. Published accounts suggest that the voluntary embargo was decidedly leaky, enabling the South African authorities to obtain equipment and supplies as well as licensing arrangements for production of goods in South Africa, though at some premium in price. The state-owned ARMSCOR was established in 1968 to promote domestic self-sufficiency in a wide range of items. While reports about its success are conflicting, ARMSCOR was exporting a number of products by the end of the 1970s. Since the implementation of mandatory sanctions in 1977, the price premium on goods and on licensing arrangements has increased; reports indicate that prices have more than doubled on some items. Producers in a number of countries—France, Germany, Israel, Italy, the Netherlands, and Switzerland—have been active in the arms trade despite the embargo. And South Africa has access to a large secondhand market in jet engines, as well as technical capacity to modernize its weaponry using technology from other countries.

Information on the effects of the boycott is not solid, since the figures on trade and details of budgets and production are not made public. In the short term, the embargo increased the prices South Africa paid for imports and made some items unavailable. Qualitatively, the pattern suggested above seems to have held. There was a period of rapid growth of the domestic industry, some success in bringing costs down to internationally competitive levels as shown by export sales, and some access to new technology on legal or gray-market acquisition of licenses. But the country faces potentially serious problems in the longer run without access to some items that cannot be produced economically at home. The arms industry may now employ up to 100,000 people in South Africa, reflecting some of the domestic benefits that come from lack of access to international markets.

ARMSCOR successes include production of the G-5 howitzer, a highly regarded weapon. A 1987 U.S. State Department study noted that many of the weapons systems manufactured in South Africa were in place prior to 1977 and have been maintained and even upgraded since then, especially systems originally supplied by France, Israel, and Italy. Present trade seems to be largely in subsystems to maintain control of final design in South Africa and to minimize detection of the trade. Some sources have reported acquisition difficulties in areas such as electronics, an essential component of modern weapons systems, and modern aircraft. However, the aging fleet of French Mirages may have reasonable prospects of being upgraded and replaced effectively, and reports of an indigenously developed fighter—the Cheetah—have been very optimistic from South Africa's viewpoint. A quarter-century after the initial voluntary embargo, and more than a decade since the mandatory embargo began, the South African Defense Force is still considered the most effective in Sub-Saharan Africa.[1]

Oil

The Arab oil-exporting countries imposed an oil embargo on South Africa in 1973. Its effectiveness increased following the fall in 1979 of the shah of Iran, who had been South Africa's major oil supplier. The oil embargo has probably been the costliest international action against South Africa to date. Pressure for an oil boycott, as well as South African planning to respond to it, had been going on for a long time. Since the boycott began, South Africa has not been deprived of oil, but it has had to pay substantial premiums, particularly in the tight oil markets of 1979–1982. In the short run, the higher prices imposed extremely high costs. Two estimates of the short-term price effects, one attributed to the African National Congress and another mentioned by President Botha in a 1986 speech, both put the costs to South Africa in the range of R22 billion since the boycott began, or $1–$2 billion annually (at historic exchange rates). This figure seems to be composed of annual price premiums and the capital costs both of SASOL and of purchasing oil stockpiles.

The South African authorities have responded to the boycott in several ways: stockpiling of crude oil; conservation; substitution of other energy sources for oil; increased exploration for oil and gas; and construction of the SASOL coal conversion plants, which make liquid fuels from coal. The boycott has involved costs to the South African economy beyond the higher price of oil in the international market. Stockpiles must be purchased. The generally accepted estimate of one to two years' supplies would mean tying up $1–$4 billion or more in capital, depending on the acquisition price. Substitution often carries higher capital or operating costs than using petroleum products, as with the electrification of the railways. The SASOL projects have been highly capital-intensive and are financially viable only because of the protection inherent in the high price of imported oil due to the boycott.

The decisions forced on South Africa by the oil boycott have resulted not only in higher costs. The SASOL projects, for example, have pushed South Africa into international leadership in coal conversion technology; and the forced march into greater self-sufficiency has had positive economic spinoffs. Policy actions by the government effectively mitigated both the economic costs and the disruption of the oil embargo, and South Africa is in a better position today to meet short-term cutoffs in oil supplies than it was a decade or two ago.

Other Trade Measures

The various packages of sanctions that have been adopted by the United States, the Commonwealth of Nations, and the European Community in recent years have changed the game for South Africa. While earlier measures had been aimed largely at denying South Africa access to supplies—of arms and oil—those adopted by the United States and other Western countries seek to deprive it of export markets as well.[2]

The buildup to the imposition of sanctions by the Western countries and the Commonwealth provided a period for South Africa to plan for bearing their impact. The registration of companies in a wide variety of countries to provide cover for purchases and sales increased. The staffs of the relevant ministries and departments in the South African government have been augmented by people with previous experience, often ex-Rhodesians. Efforts to gain access to technology in the computer field, for instance, have been stepped up so that import replacement can proceed in a systematic manner rather than at a forced pace. Contingency arrangements are being made with a variety of airlines to lease South African equipment to assure continued service to South Africa under different flags. Perhaps more important for the longer run, discussion has increased about the overall strategy for economic growth if South Africa has to face world markets over the barrier of increased economic sanctions and voluntary pressures. Finally, since the South African government is publishing less information about trading patterns, measuring and monitoring the effects of increased pressures will be harder for outsiders than it has been in the past.

It is difficult for several reasons to assess the effects of the trade sanctions adopted since 1985. The South African economy was going through a serious recession before these measures were adopted. The lagged effects of the substantial devaluation of the rand would reinforce the restrictive effects of trade sanctions on imports and counteract the effects on exports. The flow of statistical information on trade has been reduced, and it is always difficult for economic analysts to calculate the difference between what happened and what might have happened. In addition, the only distinctive products that South Africa produces, gold and strategic minerals, were little affected by the sanctions. Beyond those products, shifts of international markets could have been expected to absorb the small amounts of South African exports with relatively low price discounts. South Africa's total nongold exports amount to only about $10 billion of the total world exports of over $2.5 trillion. Nonetheless, in easily traceable items, such as coal, South Africa seems to have suffered from price discounting, albeit in an exceptionally soft international market, and to have reduced shipments after Western countries adopted restrictive measures toward its exports.

While the exercise of determining what might have been in the absence of international pressure is well beyond what can be attempted here, the data on the volume of exports do not suggest that the recent round of trade-related sanctions have had major effects. As shown in Figure 5.1, the volume of nongold exports (their real level, unadjusted for price changes) dropped by nearly one-quarter between 1980 and 1983 as the international economic recession hit South Africa's export markets. However, after the nadir in 1983, the volume increased by nearly 40

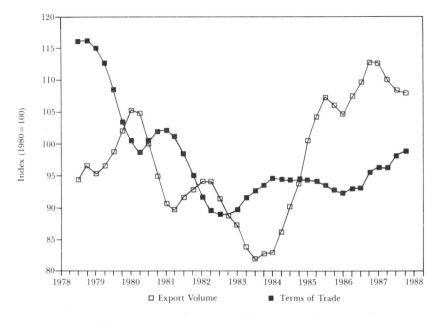

Source: South African Reserve Bank, *Quarterly Bulletin*, various issues.
*Four-quarter moving average, centered on third quarter.

FIG. 5.1. NONGOLD EXPORT VOLUME AND TERMS OF TRADE,
1978–1987*

percent to the final quarter of 1987 and continued to expand in
1988 and 1989. The terms of trade excluding gold also deteriorated sharply after 1980, dropping by 12 percent between 1980
and 1982, as the figure shows. Subsequently, the terms changed
modestly from quarter to quarter, improving slightly between
1983 and 1987. The volume of imports fell by 14 percent in 1985
and by another 3 percent in 1986, largely in response to domestic
recession, tight money, and the substantial devaluations of the
rand. Import volume rose again in 1987 and 1988. It is difficult
to read any significant effect of the trade sanctions at the aggregate economic level, even though in certain cases trade clearly
has decreased, apparently in direct response to sanctions. Examples include the total volume and value of coal exports and the
level of trade in specific commodities between South Africa and
the United States.

While the most recent international pressures may not have
produced measurable effects on the aggregate level of output or

international trade, they have affected the psychology of the business community in South Africa. Here, however, the information must be more qualitative than quantitative. It is difficult to disentangle the effects of actions by the international community from those by the South African authorities and from domestic political developments. During the time of *anticipation* of recently imposed sanctions, the authorities appeared to have lost direction, domestic violence increased in response to the 1984 constitution and the subsequent repression, and the government imposed a state of emergency. The resulting loss of business confidence was reflected dramatically in the falling level of investment and the rising rates of emigration and capital flight, as well as in a generally hostile attitude toward the government on the part of the business community, particularly its English-speaking members. As the reality and universality of international pressures began to be clear, however, the business community switched to a sanctions-busting mode of operating, while substantially muting its criticism of the government. By 1987 and 1988, business confidence had increased, a development reflected in opinion polls and in levels of economic activity. While business continues to criticize the government for its "economic laager" mentality, the private sector clearly is ready to participate in another round of import substitution to reduce South Africa's vulnerability to trade sanctions, and in measures to avoid sanctions on exports.

Finally, it is worth noting that not only is South Africa a highly managed and regulated economy, but it has been involved in purposeful import-substituting industrialization since the 1920s, and in planned rationalization of industry for most of the post–World War II period. Such industries as diesel engines for tractors and trucks have been selected for import substitution as much for their strategic importance as for their potential economic value. The authorities and the private sector have considerable experience in playing this particular game. One of the major questions for the future is, What additional goods currently being imported can be produced at home, and at what cost? Studies released by the Board of Trade and Industry and other official bodies suggest that even with the present composition of demand and development strategy, imports could be reduced by at least another 25 percent through planned import substitution. While that is probably an exaggeration, given the existing structure of the economy, potential import substitution is worth further analysis because it is a matter of critical importance for assessing future developments.

CAPITAL ACCOUNT PRESSURES

The campaign against investment in South Africa has a long history, stretching back to the early 1960s. The role of foreign capital in the early development of South Africa was critical. Even in the immediate post–World War II years, foreign capital financed a substantial share of investment in South Africa. However, ever since the beginning days of the diamond mines, the profitability of investment in South Africa has been such that a very large share of new foreign investment either has been financed by the flow of profits on earlier investments or could have been financed that way. Nevertheless, the government, considerable sections of the business community, and many opponents of the South African regime, at home and abroad, view the role of foreign capital as critical to South Africa's continued economic growth. Stopping or reversing the flow of foreign capital to South Africa has always been high on the agenda of the domestic and international anti-apartheid movement.

While pressure was placed on international firms and banks after the Sharpeville massacre in 1960, it was relatively short-lived. Indeed, the support shown by some international business figures for continued foreign investment in South Africa is often cited to illustrate the symbiosis of the South African government and international capital. The authorities blocked the transfer of equity capital from South Africa at the time of Sharpeville, and subsequently formalized the "securities rand." This instrument was designed to insulate the overall balance of payments and the level of international reserves from the effects of capital flight. The securities rand in the 1970s, and the financial rand, introduced in 1985, provided an incentive to foreign investors, who could buy rand for equity investment purposes at a favorable price.

The pressure on international companies, especially on U.S.–based multinationals, began to increase in the 1970s, most markedly after the 1976 Soweto uprising and the government's repressive reaction. In both the United States and Great Britain, and to a lesser extent in the other industrial countries, the level of interest in the South African operations of businesses and banks rose dramatically. At the same time, the state and parastatal bodies were taking on an increasing role in major investment projects in South Africa. Finally, sentiment was growing in the industrialized countries that South Africa was endangering its longer-run economic viability by continuing its apartheid policies.

Beginning in the 1960s, a combination of activist pressure, a coldly calculating view of the country's future, and the shift in domestic investment priorities led to a decline in the level of long-term capital flowing into South Africa. The composition of the remaining investment shifted toward loans, particularly to the parastatal and public sectors. By the late 1970s South Africa was having increasing difficulty even raising longer-term funds for public and parastatal borrowers. The pressure on many banks had focused on lending to the public sector, and while significant lending continued, a shift began toward lending to the private sector. These shifts were shown graphically in the preceding chapter.

International pressures notwithstanding, foreign direct investment increased in the early 1980s, almost entirely as a result of reinvestment of earnings by foreign multinationals. Private portfolio investment, always more volatile than direct investment, fell off substantially. In both cases, the investments represented only a fraction of the dividends and profits companies and individuals were earning from their South African investments: the recorded outflow of dividends and profits was much higher than the inflow of equity capital to South Africa. In the case of foreign direct investment, the outward flow of dividends and profits had been at least two to three times the inflow of new capital for three decades or more. If South Africa could acquire the assets owned by foreigners on favorable terms, it could substantially improve its overall balance of payments by simultaneously eliminating foreign investment from retained earnings and payment of residual dividends and profits abroad.

As these developments were unfolding, government policy on a variety of monetary questions was under active review. A series of reforms in monetary policy was introduced, aiming at greater freedom for market forces in a number of areas of the economy, including credit and foreign exchange markets. One major development was the 1983 abolition of the securities rand, which meant that any capital movements, in or out, would directly affect the level of foreign exchange reserves and the value of the rand. Another reform was to shift from a peg of the rand to the U.S. dollar to a managed float of the rand, with the South African Reserve Bank taking a more active role in setting the exchange rate on a day-to-day basis. Domestic interest rates were allowed to fluctuate according to market conditions, while the authorities attempted to manage the monetary aggregates more tightly, although several periods of excessive looseness in both monetary and fiscal policy added to domestic inflation. Furthermore, exchange controls on capital movements were loosened, and domestic banks and firms were encouraged to borrow abroad or at home, depending on their own judgments of interest rates and exchange risks. All these events set the stage for the debt crisis of 1985.

As the South African economy declined from the gold boom of 1980 and entered a period of excess-demand inflation and deteriorating foreign reserves over the following four years, government policies—creating high interest rates domestically, tightening money, and relaxing capital controls—encouraged the private sector to borrow from abroad, where nominal interest rates had dropped earlier than they had in South Africa. With access to longer-term foreign capital for the public and parastatal sectors increasingly limited, short-term private-sector borrowing seemed to be a sensible way of achieving some foreign capital inflow to support the overall balance of payments and the level of reserves. Short-term debt grew rapidly from 1981 through 1985.

By the middle of 1985 concern over the continuing level of violence that had begun in late 1984 caused the international business and financial community to question more sharply the longer-term financial risks of investing in South Africa. The long-running saga of the international debt problems of other parts of the world was also a factor. In July 1985, ten days after President Botha declared a limited state of emergency, Chase Manhattan Bank notified South African borrowers that it would not roll over its credits when they became due. Other banks rapidly followed suit, since none was in a position to be the last one out the door. In August President Botha scheduled a speech in which he was expected to announce fundamental political changes. In fact, the speech was a grave disappointment to those in South Africa and abroad who had been hoping for movement toward genuine democratic reforms. The financial markets reacted with a rush to the door, and on August 27 the government suspended dealings in foreign exchange and on the South African stock exchange. On September 1, the government of South Africa announced that while it would continue paying interest on its loans, it was adopting a standstill on principal payments of some $12 billion of debt, about half of the total outstanding.

In subsequent months, the government reached understandings with its creditors in the standstill net. But it was unable to reach any agreement for a long-term voluntary rescheduling and, as part of the understandings, had not received new money. In effect, South Africa told its creditors inside the net that it would pay them when it could do so. As a sign of its good intentions, it repaid 5 percent of the outstanding amounts in 1986 and scheduled similar amounts for 1987 and 1988. By 1988 it had also negotiated some shift of debt from inside the net to longer-term loans by offering a "special exit" opportunity to banks, under which they could convert their short-term debt to fixed repayment debt. However, the debt issue continued to cause concern in South Africa for both the government and the business community.

The banking crisis was probably the most dramatic crisis resulting from international pressures on South Africa. What were its effects on the South African economy and the government? And what can be learned from it?

In order to deal with the loss of confidence in the economy and counteract the capital flight that was expected from the debt standstill, the government introduced the financial rand for equity transactions. This meant that anyone wishing to purchase foreign exchange for purposes of moving equity capital out of the country has to purchase it from the financial rand pool. Foreign exchange for the pool comes from investors bringing equity capital into South Africa, and the exchange rate is a market rate, set by the demand and supply of foreign capital. The introduction of the financial rand meant that capital flight, other than illegal flows, such as those accomplished through price manipulations of imports and exports, would not affect the overall balance of payments or the level of foreign reserves.

An immediate effect of the debt standstill was that South Africa could not draw on bank loans to pay for imports. Since loans were not being repaid, banks would not lend new funds. While South Africa did not have to switch to a cash basis for all its import payments because it was able to maintain normal access for some revolving trade credits, there were large net capital outflows from 1985 to 1988. This meant that the South African government had to produce a large enough surplus of export earnings over import payments to repay creditors outside the standstill net, to make voluntary payments to those inside the net, and to build foreign exchange reserves so that fluctuations in future export earnings and import payments could be met without resort to further foreign borrowing.

The cutting off of short-term capital was a singular event that was painful to South Africa but cannot be repeated. It was, in effect, a "one-shot" measure for both South Africa and the international community. To the extent that South Africa built up sufficient foreign exchange reserves to finance fluctuations in external payments, it is in the same position it would have been in with access to short-term capital, though without the "insurance policy" of access to credit to meet emergency needs. Moreover,

South Africa can keep dealing with the commercial banks inside the standstill net on the basis that the government may pay off outstanding loans at a rate it feels is prudent.

The reactions of South Africa to reductions of foreign long-term capital, to the recession of the early 1980s, and to the 1985 crisis suggest that the government has a good deal of flexibility and a good many options. One of the most dramatic aspects of the adjustment policies has been the substantial devaluation of the rand. The abandonment of the gold standard during the Great Depression and the devaluation after World War II were powerful policy measures that enabled South Africa to outperform other economies in the ensuing periods. The devaluation in the period 1981–1986 provided a major stimulant to both import-replacement and export industries. It also accounted for a substantial share of the success in running a current account surplus, and in adjusting to both the credit cutoff and the reduction in the flows of longer-term capital. While the depreciation of the rand has undoubtedly fed the rate of inflation, relative prices and investment incentives have changed in favor of activities that either replace imports or produce exports—precisely the kinds of activities that South Africa needed to undertake.

The treatment of foreign creditors also bears mention. The authorities wanted to reach an agreement that would restore South Africa's credit ratings and make new short- and inter-mediate-term loans available as soon as possible. However, they knew that South Africa, as a major debtor, was in a stronger position than the banks in the short term. The banks would not declare South Africa in default, as this would require them to write off outstanding loans and sustain losses; it might also set precedents for other sovereign loans. South Africa continued to pay interest in order to keep loans current; in effect it told the banks inside the standstill net that it would pay principal when it could. The government used its bargaining power to good effect. As a result, it has been able to maintain some forms of trade credit, and by late 1988 it even returned to short-term borrowing from some banks.

Finally, the introduction of the financial rand is an important development, particularly in combination with the substantial devaluation of the commercial rand. On the one hand, the financial rand has insulated South Africa's foreign exchange reserves from the financial effects of disinvestment, since investors cannot take foreign exchange out unless other investors are bringing foreign exchange in. On the other hand, the very low value of the financial rand means that when disinvestment does take place, South African companies that buy the assets purchase real assets at extremely low prices. A sizable portion of such assets are being acquired by the largest domestic investors, a process that is increasing the concentration of economic wealth and power within South Africa. Also, investors who come in through the financial rand benefit by being able to take out dividends and profits via the commercial rand. If an asset pays a 15 percent return in rand terms and if the financial rand discount is 50 percent, then the asset would pay a 30 percent return in terms of foreign currency. Given the incentive inherent in the financial rand, an investor does not have to take too long a view on the South African economy to have a full return of capital. So the mechanism has provided both a penalty to investors who want to leave and an incentive to those who might consider coming in.

AN ASSESSMENT OF PAST PRESSURES

Actions by the international community have imposed a major cost on South Africa since 1974: oil costs substantially more, arms are more expensive, access to some export markets and availability of imports from some sources is restricted, the flow of foreign direct investment and long-term lending has dried up, foreigners have withdrawn investments, and South Africa is no longer welcome as a major borrower in short-term markets. The combined effects are extremely difficult to measure, but they must be in the neighborhood of several billion dollars annually in losses, from higher prices paid for imports, or lower prices received for exports, or lack of access to capital inflows to finance investment.

In addition to these immediate losses, ARMSCOR, SASOL, and oil stockpiles have involved substantial capital investments that would not have been necessary in the absence of the international boycotts. Selection of industries for import substitution would probably have been different were further actions to deny South Africa access to goods not anticipated. Finally, while I know of no solid information on the subject, the South African authorities have indicated that they have been stockpiling items other than crude oil in expectation of additional action by the international community. All these activities involve investments that yield lower economic returns than would alternative investment allocations, thus depressing rates of output growth. It is impossible to put a firm figure on this loss, or to disentangle the effects of this factor from either those of inefficiencies of the apartheid system that have slowed economic growth in South Africa or those of the softening of the international economy in the 1980s. However, it is clear from the aggregate figures shown in chapters 2 and 6 that growth rates have decelerated and productivity of new investments has decreased substantially at the same time that international pressures have increased. Had the South African economy been able to sustain its growth rates of the 1946–1975 period through the late 1980s, real GDP would have been more than 45 percent higher, and real GDP per capita would have increased rather than declined.

In assessing the overall effects of pressures on South Africa, it is important not to take too short a view. Following the adoption of various measures by countries, organizations, and the commercial banks from 1984 to 1987, many observers were quick to render judgments about whether economic pressures were or were not "working." Some short-run measures, such as the oil boycott, can and do have both immediate and long-lasting effects, though the adverse longer-term effects can be mitigated by policy choices. Other actions may have immediate effects that can be offset by policy, but may still have cumulative effects that take some time to become obvious. The intermediate-term success of ARMSCOR in providing supplies of armaments might be overcome by the longer-term inability of South Africa's arms industry to maintain its regional superiority due to lack of access to technology. A great deal of the outcome depends on the government's approach both in anticipating and in responding to actions by the international community.

Finally, the reactions of others in South Africa, particularly the black majority and whites actively opposed to apartheid, will be extremely important in determining the effects of further economic pressures, as they have been important in the events of the past three decades. The drop in business activity in the late 1970s and the mid-1980s was due at least as much to domestic responses to government racial policies and loss of confidence in the government's ability to manage the country as to actions in the international economy.

FURTHER ECONOMIC PRESSURES:
POSSIBLE DOMESTIC IMPACT AND REACTIONS

Most readers are likely to be more interested in what can be said about the likelihood and potential effects of economic pressure in bringing about change in South Africa than in any other topic that may be discussed. They may be disappointed to find that the areas of ignorance and uncertainty are exceptionally large. The intention here is to provide a framework for thinking through the issue.

The purpose of economic pressure, in very broad terms, is to impose costs on the ruling regime that will cause it to change its behavior in a particular direction. In addition, some individuals and groups are motivated simply by a wish to avoid any contact with a regime they find immoral. The effectiveness of economic pressure in bringing about a change in behavior depends on several links in an argument. First, the pressures applied must be capable of producing a reduction in real income and output. Second, this reduction must limit either the government's ability to maintain effective control over the majority of the South African population or its willingness to continue the basic features of the apartheid system, or both. While the link from higher cost and lower income to changed behavior is fundamental to the argument, this section addresses only the link between international actions and the level of activity in the South African economy.

It is important to distinguish between several issues in discussing the effects of international sanctions: between short-term income effects and long-term effects on economic growth rates; between sanctions that affect trade in goods and services, including technology, and those that affect flows of capital; between partial sanctions, which affect some imports and exports, and total sanctions, which affect everything; and between mandatory and voluntary sanctions, particularly between those that affect the behavior of virtually all countries and those that affect the behavior of only some countries. Only by taking into account these distinctions will it be possible to reach useful conclusions about the likely effects of particular sanctions on the South African economy.

Over the past decade or more, a number of estimates have been made of the effects of various types and levels of sanctions on the South African economy. These range in sophistication from back-of-the-envelope calculations of what might happen, to simple projection models based on assumed productivity of capital investment, to econometric and linear programming optimization models. Some take explicit account of possibilities for changing the economic behavior of major sectors in South Africa or the economic parameters that determine the relationships between input and output. The findings differ depending on the assumptions about the type of sanctions, the level of effectiveness, and the ability of the economy to adjust. Nonetheless, the fundamental conclusion of *all* these studies is that trade sanctions *can* damage the South African economy by reducing its level of real output and income. The critical question is, By how much?

Most of the studies hold that because of South Africa's relatively heavy dependence on imported intermediate and capital goods, a decline in the level of real imports would reduce the economy's capacity to produce goods and services domestically. A diminished volume of imports could come about by any of several means: physical restrictions imposed by exporting countries; reduced purchasing power from a given amount of export earnings due to the higher import prices necessary to overcome sanctions; decreased export earnings due to reductions in either volume or prices that would be necessary to overcome trade sanctions by the importing countries; or decreases in access to international capital to finance imports.

In the studies that have recognized some limited possibilities for import replacement,[3] the estimates suggest that for sanctions that reduce real levels of imports by up to 30 percent, real levels of GDP would fall by one-third to two-thirds of 1 percent for each 1 percent decrease in import volume. Thus, actions that reduced the volume of imports by 20 percent might cause a 10 percent reduction in real GDP (though the level might be as low as 7 percent or as high as 14 percent or 15 percent). Richard Porter is the only analyst who has looked at levels of sanctions that affect real imports by more than 30 percent, and he points out that with greater reductions in imports, the possibilities for restructuring the domestic economy become more and more difficult, thus increasing the proportionate reduction in real output that would have to take place in order to cope with a declining real level of imports.

Virtually all studies that have analyzed the effects of sanctions suggest that losses in employment are likely to be larger for black than for white South Africans, not only numerically but also in percentage terms. This certainly conforms with history, including the Great Depression, as well as with the effects of more recent events.

Most analysts have concluded that the amount of "damage" trade sanctions can do is limited to something in the range of a 30 percent reduction of the real level of imports or, equivalently, the purchasing power of exports. The main reason is that it would be exceedingly difficult to enforce sanctions against South Africa's gold and diamond exports,[4] and the strategic minerals are unlikely to be included in any sanctions package agreed to by Western countries. Thus, 50–60 percent of exports would likely not be affected at all by total sanctions. On the import side, while significant price effects on such commodities as oil are clearly possible, most analysts suggest that sanctions against exports to South Africa are likely to be leaky. Such actions would be partial rather than total, if voted by the UN Security Council, and would probably not involve all commodities for all countries. Thus, though the South African economy might sustain substantial damage through a large reduction of the real value of imported commodities and services, real import volumes are not likely to decline by more than one-third.

It should also be noted that the effects of sanctions depend very much on the level from which they begin. Porter makes it clear that the government can *anticipate* sanctions and make preparation for them in order to reduce both their short- and intermediate-term effects. The ability of the South African economy to respond to reductions in the real level of imports depends on the point in the economic cycle at which sanctions are initiated. For example, effective sanctions imposed at the end of 1986, when the real volume of imports had already declined by more than 25 percent over five years, presumably would have had a much greater impact on the level of real output and employment than a similar level of sanctions adopted at the peak of the gold price boom. Thus, the short-run effects are extremely difficult to predict, even assuming that policy measures are constant.

One major point of emphasis in all studies of the effect of sanctions is the importance of South African policy response. Two particular elements of policy response bear attention. The first is import replacement. Since the principal impact of sanctions on real income is through the denial of "necessary" imports, the question arises, How rigid are the demand parameters for imports, and how quickly can those parameters be changed? Since many import-substitution industries in South Africa developed on the basis of imported intermediate goods and semi-processed raw materials, they are relatively dependent in the short run on imported goods to sustain production. The difficult and important question is, If policy required it, how quickly could import replacement at reasonable costs take place?

The second question regarding policy response is related to the acceptance of constraints in the overall economic system, particularly the issue of protecting levels of white employment and income. Implicitly or explicitly, the sanctions discussion emphasizes either reducing levels of white economic welfare to the point where the white electorate or its government feels that the time has come for serious negotiation, or reducing the ability of the authorities to control the nonwhite population and white opponents of the regime. To the extent that the government leaders and their constituents are willing to accept substantial changes in the allocation of resources (and thus, start with dry swimming pools, deteriorating levels of performance of BMW and Mercedes-Benz automobiles, and so forth), the "requirements" for imported intermediate and capital goods could change substantially even in the short run. And taking a longer view, the government could even make a substantial change in the overall economic strategy that would affect the composition of domestic demand and investment, as well as the import coefficients for the economy.

The effects discussed above are all short-term ones. What about the longer-term effects of sanctions on economic growth? Fewer analysts have attempted to measure this, though the recent effort by Hayes presents an interesting starting point.[5] He accepted the commitment of the South African government to pay off its external debt at the pace accepted by the commercial banks agreed to in early 1987, and assumed that no new capital would flow into the country. On the basis of his assumptions about ratios of added output to new capital investments, he suggests that the rate of output growth would fall to near zero over a five-year period. However, the government's own statements suggest that growth could continue at something in excess of 3 percent annually in real terms without foreign capital inflow, a figure that would entail very little per capita increase in real output and rapidly rising levels of black unemployment.

But what does longer-term growth look like under trade sanctions and no new investment? For several decades domestic saving in South Africa has amounted to 25 percent or more of GDP, a respectable level by international standards. The declining productivity of new capital investment over the past decade has meant that even though the ratio of investment to GDP has been high until quite recently, the rate of output growth has fallen substantially. Suppose South Africa were able to return to the average productivity of gross capital investment that it maintained for the first 30 years after World War II (about 20 percent). It would then be possible to grow in real terms at 4–5 percent annually even with no capital investment from abroad. Trade sanctions that cut 30 percent off the real level of imports might reduce real GDP by 20 percent in the short term. *If* the authorities could maintain these other historical parameters, a 4–5 percent rate of real economic growth would restore the presanctions level of real GDP within four to five years. While this is hardly a scenario a government might wish on itself, it is not outside the realm of possibility, given the relevant economic magnitudes in South Africa.

None of the studies, however, deal with what are probably the most important issues in the response of South Africa to increased economic sanctions from abroad. There have been no investigations of how much whites are willing to have their incomes lowered before their perceptions of the need for political change are modified. There have been no estimates of the effect of sanctions or of less economic growth on immigration or emigration. There have been no evaluations of the impact of sanctions on the level of investment by domestic companies. There have been no assessments of how rising black unrest and consequent disruption will influence economic performance. There have been no analyses of how reduced living standards and rising unemployment among blacks will affect organized black labor or other identifiable pressure groups in the black communities.

What conclusions may be drawn from the available information? To the extent that external efforts remain bilateral or voluntary, the increase in trade sanctions will have some "nuisance value"—some loss in the terms of trade for South Africa through increased import prices or decreased export prices— but they will not carry severe economic costs. They will most likely continue to be aimed at items that fit the interests of the countries imposing them. For example, South African coal exports will be targeted by the United States and Australia, themselves both coal exporters; and iron and steel imports from South Africa will be banned by the United States and the European Economic Community, where the steel industries are in desperate shape. South Africa will respond by rechanneling exports through other countries to hide their real origin and will pay a penalty in price and probably in quantity, but will not be seriously damaged. Most South African exports will be ignored. Gold, diamonds, and strategic minerals are unlikely to be seriously affected by sanctions. Many of South Africa's other exports are relatively homogeneous commodities and can be sold unbranded in world markets. Even coal, which, as a high-bulk, low-value commodity, might well be the object of increased trade sanctions, will become more valuable on the international market as energy prices improve in the 1990s. Multilateral and mandatory sanctions will probably remain at a level of the lowest common denominator, excluding strategic minerals, gold, and—considering the most recent behavior in the European Community—coal, too. In sum, the estimates that serious trade sanctions are likely to affect only 30–40 percent of South Africa's exports are probably in the right order of magnitude. That serious damage could be imposed is clear; that the effect would be fatal in the short or intermediate term is not at all certain.

With respect to sanctions against exports to South Africa, the wide variety of individual products and potential alternative supplies suggests that, as in the case of Southern Rhodesia, the principal effect of more comprehensive and mandatory sanctions would be to increase the premium paid by South African importers. Sanctions-busting is a profitable business, and the most likely impact would be to raise prices and remove from South African import lists easily identifiable branded products that contain specific technologies. According to both press reports and statements by South African government officials, work is well along to secure access to higher-technology products and processes in anticipation of further economic sanctions. South Africa's vulnerability may in one sense be higher than was Rhodesia's, because the latter could be supplied in a relatively anonymous way by South Africa. By contrast, South Africa will have to buy and sell largely by ocean trade, which is considerably more visible.

With regard to sanctions on capital investment, South Africa has for some time been denied access to markets for long-term capital for direct investment, for medium-term bank loans, and for publicly quoted debt instruments, and it effectively has been out of the short-term market, except for trade credits, since 1985. The disinvestment by foreign direct investors is reducing foreigners' claims on South African flows of profits and is doing so on terms that are extremely favorable to South Africa. Little discussion has taken place internationally on ways to prohibit private portfolio investment in South African stocks and shares by foreigners operating in certain relatively unregulated securities markets. But this investment has not been a major source of capital for South Africa for at least a decade. Thus, any action by the international community aimed at banning the flow of new capital to South Africa would in effect be codifying the status quo. Given that the status quo arose from voluntary action rather than government policy in Western countries, this might be a desirable thing to do. Furthermore, given the anonymity of international capital markets, South Africa would likely continue to have access to trade credits and to flows of capital for quoted shares of companies on the Johannesburg Stock Exchange even in the face of relatively comprehensive and mandatory sanctions.

THE REGIONAL IMPACT OF FURTHER PRESSURES

Regional integration and interdependence between South Africa and its neighbors is a century old. The share of South Africa's trade undertaken with SADCC countries is substantially smaller than the share of SADCC trade accounted for by South Africa. Large portions of the total foreign trade of SADCC states, excluding Angola and Tanzania, pass through South Africa. Some 350,000 nationals of SADCC countries are legally employed in South Africa, and two to three times that number are working in South Africa illegally or on a seasonal basis. With the vast majority of the region's GDP and foreign trade, transport capacity, and energy sources, South Africa is in a strong position to impose costs on the SADCC countries through sanctions, while the reverse is much less plausible. Indeed, through military action and various trade and transport sanctions, South Africa has already imposed extremely heavy costs on the SADCC members.

On the other hand, South Africa is a net beneficiary of its relationships with the SADCC states in financial terms. According to the most recent estimates available, South Africa's net foreign exchange earnings from its economic relations with these countries probably total $1.5 billion per year or more. In South Africa's current financial circumstances, it is using this exceptionally valuable flow to build its international currency reserves and repay its foreign debt.

What is the position of SADCC in the face of substantially increased sanctions against South Africa? Again, distinguishing between the short-run and the long-run effects is important. In the short term, it is in South Africa's interest to maintain its trading relationships with the SADCC countries. As indicated earlier, the main effect of economic sanctions against South Africa will be to reduce its capacity to import. South Africa's net foreign exchange earnings from its dealings with the SADCC countries would become increasingly valuable as sanctions from the rest of the world were increased. One rand of added export earnings may generate three to four rand of additional income and output in South Africa, according to government figures. However, as incomes are lost and employment among blacks declines in the face of sanctions in the short term, South Africa will doubtless face pressure to continue reducing the employment of SADCC nationals. Therefore, South Africa could be expected to repatriate some SADCC nationals. However, South Africa could also be expected to sell goods more aggressively to the SADCC states. As economic sanctions against South Africa continue to "bite," the authorities could let the rand depreciate relative to other international currencies, raising the competitiveness of South African exports and giving the SADCC countries more favorable terms in their international trade. Thus, in the short term, economic sanctions against South Africa might even benefit the SADCC countries.

This conclusion could change dramatically, of course, should the SADCC members themselves decide to impose trade restrictions against South Africa. Clearly, these countries would find it extremely difficult to switch their source of import supply and the destination of some of their exports from South Africa to other countries, given current transport arrangements. South Africa has managed a near stranglehold on the transport systems of the SADCC countries, having directly or indirectly (through support of armed opposition groups in Angola and Mozambique) destroyed the transport routes that had been used through the mid-1970s. In order for the SADCC states to have freedom of choice in their trade policy, the transportation routes through Angola, Mozambique, and Tanzania must be rehabilitated to allow them to carry significant shares of SADCC country trade once again.

The longer-term regional prospects under further economic sanctions against South Africa depend very much on overall developments in the country itself. To the extent that South Africa remained a reliable transporter and supplier of goods and services as sanctions against it were tightened, the SADCC countries might have relatively little to worry about in economic terms unless they imposed extensive sanctions against South Africa on their own. On the other hand, if South Africa's economy and security situation deteriorated, as surely they must over the long run, the SADCC states would suffer as transport routes for their imports and exports were increasingly disrupted, as their nationals were returned home from a decaying South African economy, and as the reliability of the supply of goods and services from South Africa decreased. The only way to minimize these costs in the longer run is for the SADCC countries to restore reliable transportation routes that give them an alternative both for transportation and for sources of supplies of goods and services.

All this is conditioned, of course, on South Africa's continuation of its general regional strategy: maintaining SADCC's trade and transportation links through South Africa; the corollary of disrupting SADCC transportation routes through Angola, Mozambique, and Tanzania; encouraging trade with the SADCC countries; and continuing to deny effective bases for the liberation forces in SADCC territories. There is no reason to think that South Africa's strategy will change in the face of increased sanctions by countries outside the region. Actions by countries within the region that frustrate this strategy are likely to be met with hostile responses from the South African government. However, the 1988 agreements between South Africa, Angola, and Cuba, which provide for the independence of Namibia and the withdrawal of Cuban forces from Angola, suggest one might hope for a less belligerent South African strategy in the region.

6

APARTHEID, ECONOMICS, AND POLITICAL CHANGE

The relationship between political development and economic performance is another of the most vigorously debated issues concerning South Africa and apartheid. The attempt to resolve the historical controversy surrounding the connection between the development of capitalism and the emergence of the apartheid system is beyond the scope of this book. Instead, this chapter concentrates on the aspects of that controversy that are most directly relevant to the contemporary policy debate.

APARTHEID AND ECONOMIC PERFORMANCE SINCE 1970

The 1970s marked an important economic turning point for South Africa. As it entered the decade, the South African economy, burdened by the need to preserve apartheid, was already heading for problems. In the mid-1970s it came under new pressure as a result of the unexpected outbreak of nationwide unrest following the Soweto student protests of 1976. Overall economic performance as measured by the growth of real GDP began to decline substantially during this period (see Figure 6.1). Had South Africa been able to achieve from 1975 to 1987 the growth rate it experienced between 1946 and 1975, the 1987 real GDP would have been 45 percent higher than it actually was. The bulk of this difference can be attributed to the economic burdens created by apartheid and the effort to preserve white domination.

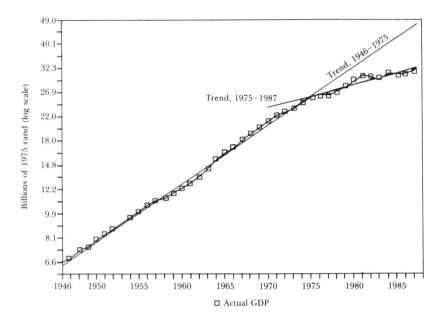

Source: Actual GDP figures from National Accounts tables of the South African Reserve Bank, *Quarterly Bulletin,* various issues.

FIG. 6.1.   ACTUAL AND TREND GROWTH, REAL GDP, 1946–1975 AND 1975–1987

The sharply lower growth trends in the period since the mid-1970s cannot be attributed to adverse changes in international market conditions. A fundamental change in the international economy took place with the freeing of the gold price in 1971 and the move to floating exchange rates for the major international currencies in 1973. Another major shift occurred with the oil shock of 1973, followed by the OPEC boycott of South Africa and, later, by the oil shock of 1979. South Africa gained substantially from the freeing of the gold price, but suffered from the effects of the oil price increase and, particularly, from the need to purchase oil at premium prices because of the boycott, especially after the fall of the shah of Iran. The gold price and oil price changes by themselves would have produced a net benefit to South Africa because of the relative importance of gold exports to oil imports.

In the 1980s international pressure on South Africa escalated, reducing access to international capital markets, first for long- and then for short-term capital, and increasing the number of products South Africa had difficulty buying or selling in some markets. Even so, the country's external terms of trade, including gold, were better in the 1970s and 1980s than they had been in the 1960s: the international recessions of the 1970s and 1980s did not damage South Africa as they did other primary producers, in part because of the unusual mix of primary commodities (notably gold, but also diamonds, strategic minerals, and coal). In short, throughout the 1970s and 1980s, domestic productivity in South Africa declined despite relatively favorable international economic conditions. Further, the share of investment in GDP was higher in the 1970s and 1980s than it had been in the 1950s and 1960s. The chief source of blame for poor economic performance must, therefore, be in the internal efficiency with which resources were used.

The dual nature of the South African economy is quite different from the dual economy one normally finds in developing countries, even those of upper-middle income. The economy no longer has a sizable traditional agricultural sector that provides an economic base for large numbers of rural people, nor a large "informal" or small-scale industry or service sector to provide a transition from the traditional to the modern sector. The homelands policy, derived from the concept of native reserves and enforced through controls on movement and settlement of blacks, has created labor reservoirs, but it has destroyed the traditional subsistence sector. The normal mechanism of economic development, which involves the shift of people from low-productivity traditional to higher-productivity modern-sector activities, has been frustrated by the development of a white high-wage class and, more recently, by the creation of a higher-wage labor elite among a minority of blacks in both the public and the private sectors. While South African commentators often say they have "First World and Third World" economy and peoples, this is neither an adequate nor an accurate description of the economy. South Africa's dual economy is much more sharply divided and lacks the basic mechanisms by which other economies have achieved sustained structural transformation.

Initially, the migrant labor system, the accompanying controls and policies, and the wage discrimination that South Africa supported did not appear to have an adverse effect on overall growth of its economy. In fact, the system may have increased the growth rate during earlier decades. By the 1970s, however, the rigidities imposed by apartheid—in labor movement; wage rates; restricted upward mobility; and access to education, training, and skill development—began to raise costs for many sectors of the modern economy. In the 1960s and early 1970s both the manufacturing and, increasingly, the mining sectors began to see the economic advantages of a settled labor force over one based on contracts and temporary migration. Erosion of job reservation gained favor among employers. As the numbers involved in migration and commutation grew, the aggregate costs in time lost and in transport expenditures that were attributable only to apartheid legislation were affecting overall levels of productivity. The manufacturing sectors complained that the legal restrictions on labor were adding to the capital intensity of their operations. And, as the small domestic market was filled with relatively high-cost import substitutes, its failure to expand with the increasing black population meant the inability to achieve economies of scale in manufacturing.

In the 1970s, the economic costs of preserving apartheid in the face of growing international isolation also began to become more apparent. Beginning with the voluntary UN arms embargo of 1963, South African authorities realized that they were likely to face growing economic restrictions. The threat that international supplies of key items, such as arms and oil, might eventually be cut off caused officials to undertake several major investment projects—including the development of an indigenous arms industry and an ambitious coal gasification scheme—that would have otherwise made little economic sense. On balance, economic performance has almost certainly suffered because of noneconomic decisions concerning resource allocation made necessary by the drive for military self-sufficiency. The SASOL coal gasification plants were developed to reduce South African vulnerability to oil embargoes. Under normal market conditions the SASOL plants would not be viable. Strategic calculations also caused South Africa to encourage import substitution in certain domestic manufacturing industries despite the likelihood of continued high costs. These investments have meant that South Africa has been devoting increasing amounts of resources to uses that result in less and less productive output, which is part of the economic price paid to maintain apartheid.

In addition to these economic inefficiencies in a narrow sense, apartheid has imposed other costs. The costs of the home-lands as duplicate administrative structures, and as attempts to buy off a black elite, were discussed earlier, as were the decentral-ization policies and incentives. Increasing domestic unrest caused by repressive legislation and regulations, as well as heightened activity from the South African liberation move-ments, led to increased budgetary allocations for defense and internal security. Mandatory military service for young white males added to the real costs, since their lost earnings were not reflected in their military pay. Defense expenditures rose from less than 1 percent of GDP in 1960 to nearly 5 percent by 1980. Defense, homelands expenditures, and related public-sector spending, including the belated attempt to do something about black education, pushed up government expenditure. Table 6.1 shows that government current expenditures rose steadily from an average of 14.0 percent of GDP in the late 1950s to 24.7 percent of GDP in the mid-1980s. Of the total increase of real GDP between the late 1950s and the early 1980s, over 30 percent was devoted to increased government spending. Since these

TABLE 6.1. GOVERNMENT CURRENT EXPENDITURE
AS PERCENTAGE OF GDP*

Period	Percentage
1947–1951	15.1
1952–1956	14.2
1957–1961	14.0
1962–1966	15.6
1967–1971	17.4
1972–1976	18.9
1977–1981	21.8
1982–1986	24.7

Sources: South African Reserve Bank, *Quarterly Bulletin,* various issues.

* Percentage is at current prices; GDP is at factor cost.

increases added little to the productive capacity of the economy, an extremely large share of added income was wasted from an economic point of view.

While the above factors were affecting productivity, investment did not fall dramatically as a share of national income until the recession of 1981–1986. The combination of continued relatively high rates of investment and growing inefficiencies of the economy produced a dramatic decline in the productivity of new investment and an associated fall in the rate of growth of GDP (noted earlier in Table 2.2). Table 6.2 and Figure 6.2 provide some rough estimates of the investment requirements per real rand of additional GDP, or of incremental ratios of capital to output since 1946. The inverse of these ratios would represent the productivity of investment in contributing to increased GDP. What is clear is a continuous rise in investment requirements, or a continuous decline in the productivity of investment, from the late 1950s through the 1980s.[1] Even discounting the exceptional

TABLE 6.2. REAL INVESTMENT REQUIREMENTS PER RAND OF ADDED
GDP SINCE WORLD WAR II*

Period	Investment per rand
1946–1956	4.55
1951–1961	4.72
1956–1966	3.71
1961–1971	3.83
1966–1976	6.13
1971–1981	10.36
1975–1985	13.78
1976–1986	29.96

Source: Calculated from South African Reserve Bank, Quarterly Bulletin, various issues.

Note: Real investment is assumed to produce increased real GDP two years later. Gross domestic investment and GDP are both measured in constant prices. Several methods of calculation produce similar results. Those reported sum real investment over five years and divide the result by the increase in real GDP over a five-year period lagged two years (e.g., if investment in 1946 produces increased income in 1948, then the investment in 1946–1950 will produce the total increased GDP in 1948–1952). This procedure produces one coefficient. Ten such coefficients are then averaged to reach the figures reported. The extremely low total increase in real GDP in 1981–1986 produces the extraordinarily high coefficient for 1976–1986.

* Ten-year average of coefficients calculated for five-year periods.

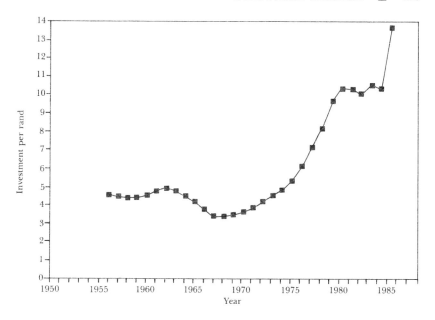

Source: Calculated from South African Reserve Bank, *Quarterly Bulletin*, various issues.
*Five-year averages, two-year lags.

FIG. 6.2. GROSS INCREMENTAL CAPITAL OUTPUT RATIOS*

data for the decades ending in 1985–1987, which are affected in part by the growing underutilization of capacity during the recession, it is clear that the upward trend in capital/output ratios, and the corresponding decline in the productivity of investment, has continued for a considerable period.[2]

Thus, leaving aside the effects of international pressures, the essential economic drawbacks inherent in apartheid have long been taking their toll on the South African economy. Many of the economic reforms introduced by the government—the liberalization of labor markets, bankable title in urban areas for black South Africans, increased educational expenditures and changed curricula for black schools, virtual elimination of job reservation—were aimed at remedying the situation. But the basic characteristics remain, despite economic and a few political reforms. The lessons Hoernle drew in the 1930s should be even more obvious today. The South African economy is too far advanced to be able to sustain apartheid. A more widespread and meaningful set of political changes and economic reforms must be put in place, or repression will increase and the economy will continue to decline.

ECONOMIC GROWTH AND POLITICAL CHANGE

A critical point of controversy in the policy debate concerning South Africa is the relationship between economic growth and political change. Will economic growth facilitate fundamental political change? Or will it simply provide resources to maintain the complex and costly system of apartheid? This controversy forms an important part of the discussion of the pros and cons of increased economic sanctions against South Africa. Will economic decline, which could be hastened by greater pressure, accelerate reform either by changing the minds of ruling whites, making it impossible for them to rule effectively, or by generating sufficient black unrest to topple the government? Or will economic decline hinder progress toward genuine reform either by increasing whites' insecurity and fears of lowered living standards and thus making them more resistant to changes, or by reducing the economic bargaining power of black South Africans and forcing them to acquiesce in order to survive?

That economic growth facilitates political reform is argued from several angles. One view is that rapid economic development, which pulls more and more black South Africans into the modern economy, will break down barriers: more blacks and whites will work together, and the scarcity of skilled labor will necessitate upgrading black workers' responsibility. This process, the argument goes, will change white attitudes toward blacks, bring blacks into contact with whites as equals in the workplace, and accelerate the reform process from the white side. A corollary to this argument is that economic growth will make it possible to improve conditions for blacks at no cost to whites, which will make whites more amenable to fundamental political changes. Another corollary is that a growing number of black South Africans holding modern-sector jobs or owning businesses will enlarge the base of people who have a stake in nonrevolutionary political change and thus increase the likelihood that political change will be peaceful.

A slightly different view of the relationship between economic growth and political change holds that greater economic power for blacks will increase their political power by making unions more influential, expanding the potential effectiveness of boycotts, and giving black South Africans a generally higher economic and political profile in dealing with whites in all forums. This view puts more emphasis on the active role of blacks in accelerating, or forcing, the pace of reform. Such reform might well take place in a confrontational milieu and might involve tough bargaining, but it would be nonrevolutionary.

The evidence to support these arguments is fragmentary. It seems clear that rapid economic development has led to a greater absorption of blacks into all sectors of the modern economy. The job status of black workers improved somewhat during the decades of rapid growth. And many observers comment that attitudes of some whites have changed slightly as a result of increased workplace integration with blacks over the past few decades. Historical trends, however, tend to weaken the argument. The period of most rapid economic growth, in the 1950s and 1960s, coincided with the consolidation of the basic elements of the apartheid system, some of the worst political repression, and an increase in white per capita income relative to black. On the other hand, "reform" in some apartheid institutions and practices—such as the new labor policies toward unions, reduced restrictions on movements of black South Africans, increased expenditure on black education and training, and the abolition of most legal job reservation—as well as the substantial narrowing of the gap between black and white wage and income levels has taken place in the context of the relatively stagnant economy since the early 1970s.

Arguments that economic pressures and decline will bring about change are also subject to conflicting historical evidence. On the one hand, it seems quite clear that during periods of substantial economic decline—in the early 1920s, in the early years of the Great Depression, and in the recession of the 1980s—government policy shifted the major burden of economic adjustment to black South Africans, principally through preferences in employment and layoff decisions that maintained jobs for whites at the expense of blacks. On the other hand, in the recession of the 1980s the government decided to make major increases in spending for black education and training despite a decline in real GDP per capita.

Simple arguments about the relationship between economic growth and political change are just that—simple arguments. In any real situation the relationships are bound to be more complex. Both black and white South Africans—and people everywhere else—have values that transcend economic welfare: political and religious beliefs, concerns about physical and psychological security, and feelings of self-esteem and a sense of self-worth are all important in determining behavior. Consequently, while one can make a logical case about how and under what conditions economic growth, or economic decline, could be the handmaiden of political change, the notion that there are direct and simple links is, quite simply, nonsense.

If the South African government were committed to fundamental political change, and *if* the majority of South Africans believed that commitment, *then* rapid rates of economic progress would smooth the road to political change by minimizing conflicts over economic issues. It is easier to deal with difficult distributive issues—of which South Africa has more than its share—if the total size of the cake is increasing. And it is easier to make changes in economic structure—accommodating the relative decline of some industries and occupations with minimum layoffs or closures—when total demand and total employment are expanding. An expanding economy would make possible more rapid advancement of blacks without major reductions in the economic welfare of whites. But it should be clear that economic growth can only ease the process of political change, it cannot cause change, although experience seems to indicate that economic progress that keeps whites in a highly privileged position reduces their perceived need for political change even on the basis of their own long-term self-interest.

If noneconomic considerations were not a factor in political behavior, then economic decline that was clearly and demonstrably related to the maintenance of apartheid institutions (whether through externally imposed pressure, the inherent inefficiencies of apartheid, or both) would lead the ruling whites to conclude that fundamental political change was necessary in order to maintain their own economic position. But what if noneconomic issues, including personal and family security, are of paramount importance to whites as well as to those blacks who have been drawn into the system? Then there is no reason to expect economic decline by itself to hasten political change; and, to the extent that economic decline worsens the internal security situation, as it might through rising black unemployment and associated unrest, it might even inhibit the pace of political change.

None of the economically deterministic processes associating economic conditions with political change makes much sense standing alone. Even if the economic case were strong, the processes would be likely to work themselves out only over relatively long periods of time, unless small changes in economic well-being evoked large changes in political behavior, which seems quite unlikely. Economic pressure can no doubt impose a variety of costs on South Africa, and they have done so already. But neither the link between the short-run costs and economic growth nor that between economic growth—or decline—and political change is strong and direct. If these arguments are correct, then *both* simple pro-sanctions *and* simple anti-sanctions positions, which project substantial and relatively rapid effects of economic change on the pace of political change in South Africa, are off the mark. The systems involved are much too complex to be subsumed in such simple models.

As stated in chapter 5, I believe that economic pressure is an appropriate instrument of foreign policy. They should doubtless be a part of U.S. and other efforts to influence the conduct of the South African government. What is called for is a clearer understanding of the likely *economic* impact of pressure in the short and long run, and the linking of specific objectives with the application, and the lifting, of specific types of pressure—something that has not been a part of the process to date. Further, since South Africa's trade and investment patterns are both so dispersed internationally, any effort to use economic pressure effectively will depend, I think, on the ability of the major Western countries to agree on sanctions measures and enforcement.

ECONOMIC PROSPECTS UNDER CONTINUED WHITE RULE

Speculating about South Africa's future economic performance is risky business. In the absence of an end to apartheid, however, it is difficult to envision anything but economic decline—characterized by depressed growth, lowered living standards, and heightened competition for increasingly scarce resources. As the following pages demonstrate, the rate, shape, and extent of decline will depend on a number of factors, including the kinds and levels of additional international pressures that develop, the economic strategies South Africa's rulers choose to pursue, and, most important, the scope and intensity of repression, unrest, and violence in the country.

Over the past decade the South African government has pursued a policy of limited political reform, which has so far involved changing the formal institutional basis of political control and reducing restrictions on racial interaction and black participation in the economy. But the fundamentals of apartheid remain in place, demonstrating the government's determination to keep political and economic control in white hands. Economically, reform has meant increasing shares of income to employed black individuals; encouraging the emergence of a black middle class with a stake in "the system"; decentralizing industry to less-developed areas within South Africa, especially the homelands, to minimize the pressure for black migration into existing urban-industrial areas; increasing blacks' access to skills and education; and reducing controls over movement of labor to jobs throughout South Africa.

South Africa has changed its overall economic strategy relatively little over the past 50 years. It has been a primary-product exporter, with industrialization based principally on import substitution behind substantial protective barriers and exports of manufactures mainly to regional markets. The result has been the continuing shift in the composition of imports toward intermediate and capital goods, and a vulnerability of domestic output, employment, and investment to interruptions in the flow of imports. Despite considerable government rhetoric about the private sector, the latter has been tightly controlled, and the government and parastatal sectors have accounted for a substantial and increasing share of economic activity. The focus on primary exports has affected the demand for various kinds of infrastructure, including transportation and electric power, and these sectors, as well as capital-intensive large-scale mining developments, have contributed to both the import intensity and, especially, the capital intensity of recent increases of GDP. Finally, the strategy has involved increasing commitment of resources to defense and security expenditures and, more recently, to education and training to make up for the massive neglect of the black community over the past 40 years. This policy mix has become progressively unsustainable.

In the absence of fundamental political change, South Africa is likely to face an ever more adverse international economic environment. As long as apartheid remains in force, the best Pretoria can hope for is that economic pressure grows slowly, hesitantly, and in an uncoordinated manner. This would mean continuing restrictions on access to international capital; increasing restrictions on exports to all countries, especially on manufactured goods, agricultural commodities, and nonstrategic minerals, such as coal; and greater restrictions on exports to South Africa, particularly on products involving higher levels of technology and on goods and services that could be utilized by the government and by the security establishment. Under this set of developments, the volume and price of South Africa's imports and exports would experience a year-by-year squeeze, producing a measurable but not dramatic deterioration in the external terms of trade compared with what they might have been without sanctions. As long as pressures remain limited, South Africa will be able to circumvent sanctions, but at a cost. Its access to short-term trade credits will probably improve, since financing sanctions-busting activities is likely to be a profitable business.

If international pressures escalate slowly, South Africa

might be able to achieve some economic growth, perhaps as much as 3–4 percent annually in terms of GDP. But the attainable level of growth would not be enough to satisfy the intensifying demand for public expenditures in areas such as internal security, defense, maintaining the homelands, and increasing real income, employment, and educational opportunities for blacks. These objectives would require growth rates similiar to those of the 1945–1975 period. For such levels to be reached, either the productivity of new investment or the rate of capital formation—probably both—would have to increase substantially. Neither is likely, given existing economic policies and rising international pressures. A change of economic strategy would therefore seem necessary and inevitable, even if increases in international economic pressures were limited.

It is also possible, however, that pressure will intensify much more rapidly and seriously. Acting in concert or through the United Nations, the major Western powers could adopt a coordinated package of trade and investment sanctions that would be much more difficult and costly for South Africa to evade. However, it is unrealistic to assume totally effective sanctions on exports. Limits on gold exports would be either exempt or relatively easy to evade; sanctions on diamond exports would bring at best modest price reductions; and the chance of a mandatory boycott of South Africa's strategic minerals is small. On the other hand, a comprehensive ban on exports of both goods and services to South Africa, except from countries in the region, is possible. In this case, the nominal value of South Africa's exports might fall by as much as 30 percent in a short time; and, with high price premiums on imports necessary to beat sanctions, the volume of imports could well fall by 30–40 percent in the short term. Without a change in government policy, a substantial increase in international pressure could produce a relatively rapid disintegration of the South African economy and society.

By shifting to an economic strategy of "inward industrialization," South Africa might be able to improve its short- to medium-term economic prospects. It would have to recognize the importance of black consumers, adopt employment growth as a primary policy objective, focusing on increasing efficiency in manufacturing output for the domestic and the international markets, and attempt to promote economic growth by improving the level of incomes and physical infrastructure for blacks. Elements of this strategy have been discussed widely in South Africa since the mid-1980s. Since the pattern of demand for consumer goods and investment would be much less import-intensive under this strategy, the economy would be less vulnerable to external economic sanctions. The growth of demand domestically would not be matched by the growth of import demand or by the need for expanded export markets.

Such a shift of development strategy under continued modest increases in sanctions would make possible faster rates of GDP growth without generating excessive demand for imports. It would also ensure that additions to the capital stock are used more productively than they have been in the past decade or more. GDP could then grow at near the rates it did before 1975. Even accounting for the loss of a percentage point of GDP annually due to heightened international economic pressures, such circumstances could yield an increase in real GDP per capita, a larger increase in employment of black South Africans, and resources for continued growth of spending on social welfare and security. How long this process can be kept going depends, as in all cases, on what is happening to internal resistance, repression, and demands for genuine political change. However, a changed development strategy could provide a much longer period before economic stagnation pushed the costs of maintaining the system above the economy's capacity to pay for them. This period could perhaps be twice as long as the past development strategy would permit, at least a decade or two, even with rising levels of sanctions.

If a shift in the economic strategy occurred simultaneously with a rapid and effective escalation of sanctions, then, after an initial loss of income, output, and employment, the likelihood of an "exuberant" phase of import substitution and growth generated by domestic demand would be greater. How long this would last is impossible to forecast. But, given the experience of other economies undergoing swift policy changes, it could well be five to ten years of above-average GDP growth, over which time the economy would replace the losses of real income and jobs that came from heightened sanctions. Thereafter a reasonable growth rate might be maintained for another decade.

Thus, all other things being equal, the economic policies adopted by the South African government will have a major impact on its ability to cope with rising international pressure. Attempts to calculate the impact of economic pressure that do not take into account the dynamic nature of interactions between international actions and South African policy will be misleading. Economic developments and international economic pressures will influence the course of events in South Africa. They will determine in part the nature and range of options open to the government. They can raise—or lower—the costs of white intransigence. But economic factors will never be decisive.

The most important pressure on the South African government is the struggle of blacks—joined by a small, but expanding, number of whites—against apartheid and white rule. The ebb and flow of this struggle will continue to be the most critical limiting influence on the options, economic and otherwise, open to Pretoria. As this struggle intensifies, economic prospects will dim, international pressure will increase, and political alternatives will narrow.

Even under the most favorable conditions, however, the government will eventually be forced to choose between ending white rule and presiding over the disintegration of the state. Implicit in most arguments for economic sanctions is the assumption that when confronted with such a choice, South African whites will opt for change. As reasonable as this assumption seems, it is important to recognize that precious little historical evidence supports such a view. The white community in South Africa at present seems deeply divided. Some segments of it are slowly beginning to recognize the need for change, and others are determined to resist it. If presented with a choice between negotiations leading to the creation of a nonracial order and rapid economic decline, a future government might risk the latter. The costs of such a choice would be devastating. Many whites would emigrate, further entrenching the power of more conservative, security-minded whites. Divisions between blacks opposed to the system and those driven by personal ambitions or economic necessity to cooperate with it would intensify.

On three occasions—after the Sharpeville massacre in March 1960, during the Soweto revolt of June 1976, and throughout the national uprising of 1984–1986—we have caught a brief glimpse of the beginnings of a process of societal disintegration. Each time, a degree of "stability" was eventually restored. But on each successive occasion the scope and intensity of unrest was greater, the impact on white society and politics larger, the economic consequences more lasting and serious, the preparation to suppress the next outburst more intense, and the interval since the last unrest shorter. It seems clear from the evidence cited earlier that the economic losses have been due largely to internal, not international, action. It is difficult to envision what will happen if the cycle of unrest, repression, and economic slowdown continues and South Africa eventually descends into a semipermanent state of widespread turmoil and economic collapse. The best attempts to depict such a scenario come in fiction, such as *The Life and Times of Michael K.*, in which J. M. Coetzee describes a world of permanent insecurity with curfews, armed convoys and factories, and most blacks confined to labor camps. The result could be hundreds of thousands of lost lives, the destruction of the economic infrastructure, and a legacy of bitterness that might never be overcome. This is the type of outcome the Commonwealth Group of Eminent Persons feared when it warned that an irreversible process of disintegration might be set in motion unless steps were quickly taken to begin political negotiations.

My hope, of course, is that South Africa's rulers will realize sooner rather than later that economic and, more important, societal disintegration is inevitable over the long term unless apartheid is abandoned. If they also recognize that economic progress for all South Africans is possible if apartheid is dismantled quickly and with a minimum of violence, they might be more willing to get on with the business of negotiating a transition to a postapartheid society.

7

A POSTAPARTHEID ECONOMY

If the previous two chapters have been somewhat speculative, this one may be even more so. Only one thing is certain: apartheid will end at some point; demography, if nothing else, dictates that result. Beyond that, predictions of the timing and manner of its demise and the nature of the government that takes over are highly conjectural. The purpose here is to outline the problems, opportunities, and options that might be faced by *any* government in a postapartheid period, given the present structure and past performance of the South African economy. In addition, since the nature of the *anticipated* postapartheid regime and its policies will have an impact on the way in which the parties struggling over South Africa's future deal with one another, it may be useful to think about a postapartheid economy as a dynamic in the process of eliminating apartheid. The government has gone to great lengths to paint a dismal picture of the economies of Sub-Saharan Africa, particularly those of countries where white minority regimes were succeeded by independent governments. The prospect of a reasonably promising future—for whites and blacks—in a postapartheid economy might have some effect on the nature and degree of resistance to fundamental changes in South Africa's political system.

My interest is in exploring whether there is a plausible chance for a productive economy for all South Africans, and because of that I make a working assumption that a relatively quick, relatively peaceful transition away from apartheid to a broadly based, representative government is possible. This means that the drawn-out alternatives presented in the previous chapter, characterized by increased violence and repression and the emergence of an economy whose primary objective is to secure white control, would not be part of the transition assumed here. I also assume that the postapartheid government would be committed to basic political and economic reforms to remove preferential access to rights based on race, and to make accessible through any of several possible means a markedly larger share in the economic cake for those denied it in the past. Such a government could be given, or could give itself, any number of ideological labels. The assumption is that it would be interested in measurable and sustainable results and that it would want to face its problems and opportunities realistically. This is not meant to be an exercise in wishful thinking; the likelihood of a quick and relatively peaceful transition looks slim indeed. However, precisely because our images of the future influence our actions, it seems useful to engage in an exercise in futurology to see whether a brighter prospect might have a positive influence on the leaders, both inside South Africa and in the international community.

In brief, the argument of this chapter is that the end of apartheid will produce two major economic effects. First, the economy will receive a "postapartheid dividend," resulting from the elimination of the costs the apartheid system has placed on South Africa. This dividend will add perhaps $2 billion per year to real GDP in the short run (that is, through elimination of costly sanctions) and will reduce expenditures devoted to security and defense, decrease the capital costs of increased growth, and provide added international capital. Second, the end of apartheid will release the artificial restriction that the system has placed on the demand for education, health, and housing. It will also reduce the need for many bureaucratic jobs and the demand for semiskilled whites, who have held relatively highly paid positions by virtue of their race, as a result of the successes of the National Party's policies and the legacy of apartheid restrictions. While the first set of effects will provide new resources, the second set will increase demands for resources.

The history of economic and political injustice that has characterized the apartheid economy has given rise to hopes among the black majority for a substantial redistribution of income and wealth in a postapartheid economy. Redistributive measures have dominated much of the discussion among anti-apartheid forces. The argument here, however, is that the ending of apartheid is a positive-sum game. A postapartheid government *could* manage the economy so as to achieve relatively high growth rates of income and employment for black South Africans without a massive loss of wealth and income for whites, though some redistribution is both necessary and desirable for a variety of reasons. Clearly, the relative position of whites will fall, and many of the least-skilled doubtless will suffer a reduction in their absolute level of income. However, the prospects for a well-managed, highly productive, and rapidly growing economy mean that substantial improvement could take place for the majority of black South Africans if the government used a combination of the postapartheid dividend and a successful development strategy.

A vision of the future that looks attractive for both black and white South Africans could have a positive effect on the search for more peaceful and forward-looking solutions to South Africa's political and economic impasse. If such is the case, then the prospects for a quicker resolution of the current fundamental difficulties improve. The nature of an economic development strategy in a postapartheid South Africa will doubtless differ from that sketched here. However, the existence of plausible alternatives that would result in a brighter picture of the future than currently seen by most whites, both in the government and outside, should play a part in the discussions among the parties trying to find a way forward.

A NEW SET OF CONDITIONS

The new government will inherit a statist economy, marked by high levels of government activity, large parastatal organizations, and state regulation of economic activity at a highly detailed level. The levers of control will be in place, ready to be used for a variety of purposes quite different from those for which they were intended by the National Party architects or even earlier governments. A postapartheid government will face both major new opportunities and new problems. One might begin with the opportunities and benefits.

New Opportunities

The end of apartheid will bring both a substantial increase in real resources and the potential for higher income and productivity. The oil embargo and other forms of international pressures and sanctions are now imposing costs on the South African economy due to higher import prices and lower export prices; a conservative estimate of these costs is on the order of $2 billion a year. Discontinuing apartheid would end the restrictions, resulting in a pure economic gain to South Africa of the same order of magnitude.

In addition, if a transition were to take place in the circumstances of the late 1980s, the South African economy would have the opportunity to increase output by utilizing installed capacity at a higher rate than it can under existing economic pressures. These increases would occur without corresponding growth in capital investment in many sectors of the economy. Greater output and employment would be very inexpensive in terms of new capital investment, and one could expect substantially higher growth rates at existing levels of domestic investment.

The lifting of restrictions imposed on foreign capital inflows because of apartheid could have several beneficial effects. At a minimum, given South Africa's relatively low level of overall external debt, one would expect a genuine rescheduling of private debt with a commitment of new funds, as normally happens in reschedulings where the underlying economy is strong. This would release the constraint on growth now imposed by the need to repay, rather than roll over, foreign loans. In addition, South African borrowers—official, parastatal, and private—would regain access to international markets for both short- and long-term capital. How much *new* inflow of foreign capital would be realized is a matter of speculation, since a good deal would depend on the policies and programs of the new government (including whether it wanted to have new foreign private capital). As an upper-middle-income country, South Africa would have some access to funds from international organizations on relatively concessional terms, in addition to whatever it might attract from private markets. However, the ending of apartheid would provide a potential turnaround in the capital account of the balance of payments from a negative of $2–$3 billion per year to at worst a break-even position and more likely a net inflow of a similar size.

Ending apartheid would also substantially reduce the need for expenditures on defense and internal security. The exact amount and timing of the saving would rely not only on the policies of the new government and the general security situation it inherits, but also on the reallocation of both financial and manpower resources out of defense and security spending and into other areas. Reducing a defense establishment is no easy task, and changing the internal allocation of manpower away from internal security will also be a challenge. Nonetheless, it should be possible to save at least $1–$2 billion per year from the government budget, and possibly more, within a short time. In the absence of a substantial regional enemy, major hardware savings could accrue very quickly, and military conscription could end, even if substantial demobilization of the defense force and of other security services took a longer time.

The elimination of apartheid would also reduce a number of the inefficiencies of resource allocation that have been a drag on the South African economy for a number of years. These include the remnants of job reservation, restrictions on the free movement of individuals within the country, commuter and travel costs from restrictions on the residence rights of black South Africans, employment of bureaucrats to enforce apartheid legislation, and investments in strategic industries that were meant to blunt the effects of international sanctions. Many of the gains from eliminating apartheid will take some time to achieve, not only because of the lags in developing manpower skills, but also because of the necessity to reallocate individuals, opposition to job losses in some sectors of the bureaucracy, and inability to dismantle investment projects in strategic industries. Nonetheless, in a relatively short period of time rates of productivity of both labor and capital in most sectors of the economy should be able to increase, providing "free" resources from the point of view of the economy as a whole. To the extent that the increase in incremental capital costs of added output since the late 1960s can be attributed largely to the inefficiencies of apartheid, the elimination of apartheid could yield a dramatic improvement in the productivity of new investment and a consequent increase in real output.

New Demands and Challenges

A new government will be fortunate to have the additional resources just outlined, since the abolition of apartheid will release a demand for a variety of economic benefits and social services that have been restrained purely by apartheid restrictions. On the other hand, it will be obliged to wait for some of the savings that are inherent in the reallocation of human resources, particularly the reduction of superfluous bureaucrats—black and white.

A number of major short-term challenges face the first postapartheid regime. The demand for education and adequate resources for black South Africans within the educational system will probably constitute the largest single budgetary increase in the short run. The elimination of access based on race and the commitment of any postapartheid government to improving educational opportunity for all citizens will undoubtedly provide an enormous increase in the demand for financial and human resources to be allocated to the education sectors of national and local budgets. For example, raising per capita spending on African students in primary and secondary schools to only *half* the current level for white students would cost around $2 billion. This would be little different from similar pressures in postindependence Africa. Some demand for resources may be mitigated in the short term by the fact that an individual's access to one level of education requires not only that space be available but also that he or she has completed the previous level.

Such a rationing device will not limit the demand for health services, where apartheid has produced vast differences in access. Abolishing restrictions will produce a very large increase in the demand for health services and facilities on the part of the black population, which has been squeezed into overcrowded and underfunded facilities in the past. While some estimates suggest that the white system has excess capacity, it is reasonable to expect substantial growth in demand for new resources in the health sector. And, given the poorer health status of the majority of the population in South Africa relative to that in other upper-middle-income countries, improving access to health facilities must be high on the list of priorities for a postapartheid government.

In both education and health sectors, substantial political stresses will exist in addition to the economic and financial ones. Some of the change in access to services will be based on "leveling down" the quality and extent of service to the privileged whites, which may exacerbate problems with respect to emigration of whites. One might expect the development of more private sector activity in both health and education, with access based on income levels rather than simply race. Experience in Kenya and Zimbabwe suggests that an adjustment of this kind provides a safety valve of sorts for skilled whites, who can avoid deterioration of services and thus protect what they see as their families' interests without resorting to emigration.

The abolition of restricted access both to movement and to residence in different areas based on race will also generate a major shift in the demand for resources. The elimination of influx control, except for citizens of the "independent" homelands, has already accelerated the movement of black South Africans into urban areas, but the restrictions of the Group Areas Act have limited the movement into areas occupied by whites. Economic and infrastructural benefits will accrue, including saving on travel expenses for individual workers and on state subsidies. Furthermore, once the Group Areas Act and the homelands are scrapped, some pressure in overcrowded black communities will be relieved by movement into much less densely populated white communities.

An area of tension will involve the current preference given to whites in many jobs regardless of skill level, especially in government and parastatal organizations. Working-class Afrikaners, who benefited from the civilized labor policy, job reservation, and employment and wage preferences in the public and parastatal sectors, were a natural constituency of the National Party, although they seem to have shifted increasingly to the right-wing white parties in recent years. One of the greatest conflicts for a postapartheid government will arise from competition among blacks and whites of relatively equal skill levels for the jobs that require modest amounts of education and training. This problem has no easy solution. But the more rapid the growth of the overall economy, the easier it will be to create new jobs for black South Africans with minimal losses of jobs for whites.

Another potential cost in a postapartheid South Africa is that of emigration by skilled whites. This is one of the areas in which a picture of the future may have the greatest effect on developments. It is evident that the white dominance in a wide range of technical and scientific positions is nearly total, whether one looks at engineers, architects, computer programmers, doctors, accountants, or any other profession with a high level of educational attainment as an entry qualification. Experience in other African countries that went from white minority rule to independence based on a majority government shows considerable emigration—much of it, of course, to South Africa. The costs to the economies of those countries, which were far less sophisticated than South Africa's, were substantial. It is thus important to all, black and white, that the drain from emigration of the most highly skilled whites be minimized.

The problem is that the most highly skilled are most mobile and most likely to be needed, while those least likely to emigrate—for reasons of history, language, and skill levels—will be competing with black workers on an equal footing. This situation means that overall generalizations about white labor can be quite misleading and that detailed and disaggregated attention to the problem is required.

Finally, the end of apartheid is likely to increase the intensity of trade union activity, particularly with respect to wage issues. Since present unions often represent a labor elite among black South Africans—perhaps 12 percent of economically active blacks are union members—any postapartheid government will have difficulty dealing with increased industrial disputes about wage and benefit levels for those now employed in what are *relatively* high-wage jobs. While blacks have suffered relative to whites, data cited earlier show that income is more unequally distributed *among* blacks than among whites, and unionized black workers are current beneficiaries. The place of trade unions and the relative wage levels for unionized workers are likely to be major issues within black communities in South Africa, before and after the transition to a postapartheid regime.

A new government will doubtless wish to move on a number of economic issues, but progress in the short term will be slow for a variety of reasons. For instance, the distribution of education and skills among the South African population is *very* highly skewed by race and is one of the major underlying reasons for the unequal distribution of income. Such a maldistribution takes years of training to change. Therefore, while demands for changes in access to jobs will be immediate, and while removing barriers based purely on race can provide some immediate response, the development of a skill mix within the labor force that is not based largely on race will lag substantially. The racial balance will improve more quickly if significant numbers of South Africans living in exile return home.

Another important economic issue that engenders strong emotions is the extremely unequal distribution of the ownership of assets, physical and financial. The new government will have to decide on the type of redistribution it wishes, which will involve substantial conflicts, and will have to take account of the consequences of such redistribution for production and for new capital investment, both domestic and foreign. That something should and will be done is not at issue; how to make sensible policy will be the major problem.

Reducing income inequality will be an obvious objective, but achieving major changes may take some time. Further, the structure of production in South Africa, including the relative importance of different industries and the amount of capital and labor engaged in each, depends in part on the unequal distribution of income and in part on the policies of apartheid. Therefore, the abolition of apartheid will present some major adjustment questions. For example, employment in the automotive industry and its subsidiaries is dependent to a large degree on the unequal distribution of income: only those few near the top of the income distribution can afford automobiles. At a minimum some industries will have to be restructured. For instance, in the automotive sector the mixture of trucks and public service vehicles might rise, and that of private automobiles might fall. Many jobs in the service industries—luxury hotels, holiday resorts—also depend for their existence on the incomes and consumption patterns of the well-to-do. Further development of international tourism could help deal with the restructuring of demand; but, again, restructuring will be required. And profitability of investments such as the SASOL coal gasification plants depends on the premium prices South Africa has had to pay for its petroleum imports. In all cases, unwinding the effect of past policies on current and future production will be neither painless nor rapid, since human and physical resources cannot be transformed to other uses without some cost. In all cases, faster overall growth will make adjustment easier.

The bureaucracies in the public sector, both white and black, have grown substantially at the national, local, and homeland levels, and in the civilian and defense/security sectors. Any new government will wish to make fundamental changes in the way in which the country is administered, but it will also inherit an established set of bureaucracies based on apartheid assumptions. How long it will take to disentangle the current system and to put something else in its place is an open question. But, to be realistic, one would have to allow for some period of time before the whole system of public administration can be responsive to the needs and programs of a postapartheid government.

While one can outline and perhaps even estimate quantitatively the effects of many of the above items, the new government will face a number of challenges whose outcomes will depend on the attitudes, the psychology, and the responses of individuals and nongovernmental institutions. Three areas are worth mentioning. First, the private sector, particularly the domestic private sector, has undertaken a major portion of investment in South Africa. Unless there is wholesale nationalization and commitment to investment by the state, the willingness of investors to continue making major investments will depend heavily on their forecast of the policies of the new government, including its attitudes toward redistribution of existing wealth. Some of South Africa's major private investment groups have made considerable offshore investments in recent years, reflecting in part a lack of confidence in the National Party government.

Second, the attitudes of the private sector both in South Africa and abroad will have significant effects on the capital account of the balance of payments. "Confidence" in the new government would translate into relatively small amounts of capital flight and a rapid return of capital inflows for direct investment, bank lending, and portfolio investment, if that is something the new government would wish to encourage. Other outcomes, much more costly for the balance of payments and for the economy as a whole, are easy to imagine if the new government is viewed with suspicion.

Third, the efficiency and productivity both in the enterprise sectors of the economy and in government departments will have a major effect on economic performance and, therefore, on the resources available to the government to implement its programs. The new government will be able to influence attitudes toward efficiency and productivity both by its actions and incentives and by its public statements and demeanor. But it will have to take those attitudes into account as it designs both the substance and the public relations of its economic and financial policies.

KEY AREAS OF POLICY CHOICE

Many observers of South Africa have concluded that economics will be the area in which policy will founder because of irreconcilable conflicts. I do not share that view. Apartheid is a negative-sum game, reducing the resources available for the whole society. Ending apartheid is a positive-sum game, which increases the total resources available. Given realistic policies, the ending of apartheid could lead to extremely rapid economic progress for all South Africans, particularly those who have been at the greatest disadvantage during the years of apartheid rule. Such progress could take place without major reductions in the material standard of living of large numbers of white South Africans even though privilege based on color would be abolished and many whites—and probably some blacks—whose jobs or income premiums depend on apartheid restrictions and policies would be worse off.

One general issue needs to be set aside. The discussion about South Africa's future economic system—indeed, discussion of its present system—often draws a false set of dichotomies about capitalist market-oriented economic systems and socialist control-oriented ones. This is not helpful. No predominantly capitalist country is without major government intervention and some, often substantial, state ownership of assets. Likewise, all socialist countries have some private-sector activities, and most have placed increasing reliance, especially in recent years, on market mechanisms to govern the activities of state- or worker-owned firms. The critical issues involve questions about the mix: what decisions to leave to market forces; what to regulate and how to do it; and which assets should be held by private individuals, and which should be publicly owned. Ultimate objectives—about the level and growth of incomes and their distribution among citizens—can be met by many combinations of policies.

South Africa today has a large state sector and in many respects should be called a statist economy. In 1986, for example, only 43 percent of the estimated value of fixed capital was owned by private business enterprises. The remainder was owned by the public sector—19 percent by public authorities, 15 percent by public corporations, and 23 percent by general government agencies. The economy is highly regulated, as indicated by several of its characteristics: the elaborate tariff and import control structure; subsidies to various private-sector activities, especially in agriculture; marketing boards and price support systems for all major, and most minor, agricultural commodities; "rationalization" programs for industries that limit competition; and exchange controls for foreign transactions. Moreover, the apparatus of apartheid governs the movement of workers; the allocation of land, housing, and business enterprises; and access to education and social services. The South African economy is among the most interventionist and centrally directed in the world, notwithstanding much rhetoric to the contrary. The questions for a postapartheid government will be what kind of intervention is necessary, and to what ends.

Finally, since the end of apartheid will yield a dividend for the economy as a whole, it is critical that the best use is made of that unique increase in resources. One of the great failings of the oil-rich countries, including such high-income countries as the United Kingdom, was that they did not properly plan how to spend their bonanza. In South Africa such a windfall should be used for strategic purposes, and the leadership of a postapartheid society should be planning now.

Distribution and Equality

The most obvious and politically charged question of economic policy involves the distribution of economic benefits among citizens. The highly unequal distribution of the ownership of private assets, the greatly skewed distribution of income among citizens, the unequal distribution of employment opportunities in all sectors, and the inequality in access to social services mean that distributional issues will be high on the list of concerns for any postapartheid government, just as they were for the National Party when it came to power in 1948. Major interactions between policies on income and asset distribution and the overall performance of the economy also must be considered.

It may be useful to provide a taxonomy of key elements in distribution. Land ownership is one of the most visible issues, in part because of the denial of access by black South Africans both to ownership of agricultural land and to acquisition of land in urban areas for so many decades. The question of agricultural land is very complex. Unlike Zimbabwe, for example, South Africa has no widespread, small-scale agricultural activity in presently black areas that is constrained simply by limited access to land. Virtually everyone is part of the wage economy, for better or worse. Data cited earlier on the importance of homeland agriculture make the point with some force. Nonetheless, a major issue is how to redistribute the ownership of agricultural land in such a way that it contributes to the incomes of black South Africans who wish to earn a living by farming, without creating significant adverse consequences for the total level of agricultural production. Some form of purchase plan for white farms will doubtless be part of the program, as it was in Kenya and Zimbabwe. A reduction of subsidies to white farms may help the process of redistribution, although it would result in devaluing the assets that the current white owners see in their farms. Turning those assets into productive ones for black South Africans presents a major challenge. It will be easier to shift the ownership than to increase the productivity for new black owners.[1] The ownership of urban land is likely to shift toward black South Africans with relative ease under market conditions as the restrictions on land ownership and acquisition of businesses by race are eliminated, but this may do little for equalizing the distribution of wealth among blacks.

The ownership of other physical and financial assets, particularly the ownership of major foreign and domestic corporations, will present any postapartheid government with a difficult set of choices. Many opponents of apartheid regard private-sector corporations and their owners as the principal beneficiaries of much of the repressive legislation or as willing—sometimes eager—partners of the Nationalist government. For many, capitalism and apartheid are part of the same system. These perceptions will undoubtedly affect the attitude of any postapartheid government.

With regard to foreign companies and share ownership, the government has already adopted a series of policies that have in effect nationalized large sections of foreign interests. The value of the commercial rand has declined, while the financial rand's value has sunk even farther. Various macroeconomic policies have substantially reduced profitability, and companies disinvesting from South Africa are often receiving a few cents on the dollar from their original investments. This is a method that a postapartheid government could continue to use to place the ownership of assets in South African hands on favorable terms.

Domestic companies present a somewhat different problem. The high concentration of ownership in a few key mining and industrial groups, of which the Anglo-American DeBeers group is by far the largest, makes them obvious and highly visible targets for some form of nationalization. In addition, the amount of income flowing to the corporate sector as a whole, including parastatal corporations, is very sizable; pretax gross operating surpluses of business enterprises in South Africa account for 35–40 percent of GDP. Net post-tax operating surpluses, which represent the returns to shareholders after allowance for capital replacement, account for 10–15 percent of GDP. This figure gives a better approximation of what a government might gain by taking ownership from private shareholders through nationalization.

Government would have to consider whether its objective is to control the investment and production decisions of the largest corporations through legislation or regulations other than taking ownership; to shift profits from corporations to the rest of the economy by implementing tax changes, wage policies, pricing or tariff protection policies, or a variety of other devices instead of nationalization; or some mix of both. Concern about the wealth of individuals could be addressed by outright nationalization on a partial or total basis, the introduction of some form of wealth tax, or a variety of other measures. There are many ways of achieving objectives, once those objectives are set. The large domestic groups and their principal shareholders must realize that life in a postapartheid society will be rather different from what they have been used to. Even if the government is not committed to large-scale nationalization, it will be interested in directing major centers of economic power toward new objectives.

Policies on wages and employment have both direct and indirect effects on income distribution. The policies of the National Party that favored the employment of whites, and particularly Afrikaners, in the private, public, and parastatal sectors provided major economic benefits and a substantial transfer of income in favor of the party's principal constituents, who represented perhaps 10 percent of the population. The cost of these policies was borne by other sectors of the economy—that is, by black workers and, to some extent, the mining export sector. Any government that represents the majority of citizens cannot, by definition, provide for similar preferences in employment and high wages unless some sector of the economy can be "taxed" to pay for it—and in such a way that the overall growth of employment opportunities and wages is not restricted.

In recent years, the government has used large increases in black employment in the public sector to favor the homeland governments. These policies have been an increasing drain on budgetary resources, illustrating the dead-end nature of a policy to do something about employment and income distribution by operating through the government sector. Rapid growth of the enterprise sectors of the economy—those that produce goods and services for sale rather than being supported by tax revenues—will play an essential part in improving the standards of living for the majority of South Africans. This has implications not only for the limitations that should be placed on the growth of the public sector in employment and budgetary terms, but also for wage policy.

One of the most difficult issues that a postapartheid government will face is the conflict inherent in the existing wage and income structure. Obviously, whites are well paid relative to blacks, but those black South Africans who have wage employment in the modern sectors are much better off than the majority, who are unemployed or who work in white agriculture, in domestic service, or in the informal sectors in the homelands and the townships. The potential conflict between the interests of the organized labor movement and the rest of the antiapartheid movement in South Africa is considerable. Policies that raise the wages of black workers now employed in the relatively well-paid sectors would increase the costs of government services generally, raise the rates charged by parastatal bodies, and erode the competitive position of firms in the enterprise sectors that must compete in international markets (such as mining, manufacturing, and agriculture), while at the same time worsening the distribution of income among blacks. Experience in other countries suggests that the best remedy for the maldistribution of income and the position of the poorest parts of the population is a set of policies, including land reform, that generates rapid growth of employment opportunities. Adjustments should be made in wage levels for those already employed in some sectors, particularly to eliminate differentials based solely on race. However, employment growth—not short-term wage increases—should be the focus of a postapartheid government interested in long-term, sustainable progress for black South Africans.

Finally, what about the wage and salary levels of white South Africans? Racial discrimination has produced average levels of real income for whites comparable to those in Western Europe or North America. If white wage and salary levels are reduced in real terms, as they are likely to be in the short run, what will be the effect on the South African economy? Many individuals in South Africa have internationally marketable skills. Substantial reductions of their incomes could lead to increased emigration among the scarcest and most economically valuable members of the society. Such a development would retard growth of the overall economy and limit sustainable job creation.

The vast majority of white South Africans, including those with high skill levels, are likely to remain in South Africa even with some reductions in income, *provided* they are satisfied with other aspects of their lives, such as their perceptions of security and the prospects for themselves and their children. Most of us, after all, are attached to our homes and our country. If the economy in a postapartheid South Africa generates the rapid growth of which it is capable, people with high skill levels will be in substantial demand. They are likely to suffer neither major declines in real incomes nor major reductions in their levels of responsibility, which is an important part of anyone's sense of well-being. The experience of whites who remained in Zimbabwe provides some reassurance on this point. The real problem regarding white South Africans will be how to deal with those who have achieved their positions and favorable salaries because of racial discrimination. The inevitable losses in income that this group will sustain will present a significant political problem to a new government and is likely to be one of the major barriers to a relatively peaceful transition from apartheid.

Overall Development Strategy

The key to successful adjustment from apartheid to a post-apartheid society in South Africa will be the adoption of a strategy of economic development and a set of macroeconomic policies that generates rapid and sustained overall economic growth, with the increment in income used purposefully each year to create new capital and generate income-earning opportunities for the majority of the people. Several reasons lead to this judgment. First, it is easier to face distributional issues when more resources are available each year. Moreover, the more rapid the growth of employment, the more rapid will be the growth of opportunities for those in the lower end of the income distribution to participate in the modern, high-wage, high-productivity sectors of the economy. Further, increased growth with a reasonably elastic tax system would provide more public-sector revenues to support the increased demand for social services and for development of urban infrastructure that will be necessary after apartheid. Finally, faster growth of output and investment would facilitate the economy's adjustment to the new structure of demand for goods and services that would arise in a post-apartheid society.

One piece of arithmetic may make the point more clearly. Presently, the lowest 40 percent of the population in South Africa receives less than 10 percent of total income. If the economy could return to the annual growth rates in excess of 5 percent that it achieved in the 1950s and 1960s, the income of the poorest 40 percent would have the potential to double after only two or three years of economic growth, and incomes would not fall in any other part of the population. Naturally, it would be impossible to accomplish this in such a short time without a massive, and efficient, program of transfers. But the importance of the growth of resources in addressing the genuine needs of the majority of South Africans should be obvious. And it is critically important to remember that few in that lowest 40 percent are currently employed in the modern wage economy of mining, manufacturing, parastatals, or government. The poorest will not be helped by general increases in wages in the unionized sectors.

What, then, about an overall strategy of development? Given its fundamentals, the South African economy has the potential to return to extremely high growth rates. It is now fairly heavily based on exports of natural resources. The industrial sector and some parts of agriculture have been relatively highly protected and subsidized by the export of primary products, principally gold. The development of physical infrastructure has been good, the level of technology in many sectors is quite competitive with that of other upper-middle-income countries. South Africa's principal disadvantage relative to other upper-middle-income countries is the lack of investment in human resources over many decades. Any postapartheid government would have to devote considerable resources to remedying this situation within a decade.

While many strategies are possible, one example might illustrate that the promise of rapid and sustained growth is not a chimera. South Africa has the potential to perform at the level of the most successful of the NICs. In order to achieve such a record, it would have to shift its macroeconomic, exchange rate, tariff, and other incentive policies, as well as pay careful attention to its domestic wage rates and labor costs. A changing distribution of income and demand domestically in favor of the lower portions of the income distribution should generate rapid growth of demand for a range of manufactured products already produced domestically, though presently behind relatively high tariffs. If South Africa were to continue to move away from its long-term policy of maintaining a high value for the rand and using high tariffs and import controls, its manufactured goods would become considerably more competitive in international markets, something that has started with the drop of the rand for purposes of short-term adjustment since 1981.[2] South Africa will probably perform well after apartheid as an exporter of manufactured goods, without jeopardizing the continued growth of its primary exports. It already has established itself well in regional markets for many manufactured goods, and has a growing reputation for certain kinds of products in markets further afield. As the other NICs have shown, such a strategy would require continued efforts to maintain parity in technology and in quality with other upper-middle-income exporters, as well as flexibility in adjusting the composition of production and output as the structure of both international and domestic demand continues to change.

This is hardly an argument for free trade or for a general policy of laissez-faire. Virtually every high-growth economy in the past two decades has required substantial government intervention in order to raise production and productivity and to break into new export markets. Intervention is merely one possible and realistic strategy under which South Africa, with a good base of infrastructure, industrial and agricultural diversity, and mining to build on, and with excess capacity likely at the time of a change in regime, should be able to generate extremely rapid overall economic growth and structural change. In the process, the economy should be able to absorb sizable numbers of blacks into productive employment over relatively short periods of time.

ALTERNATIVE POLICY CHOICES

The sketch of strategy and policy choices drawn above does not conform to the stated strategy of any of the major antiapartheid groups struggling in South Africa, though it is consistent with the general outlines of the Freedom Charter. Little by way of clearly stated economic policy or strategy has been developed by the African National Congress, the United Democratic Front, the Congress of South African Trade Unions, or other major organizations. Abundant evidence throughout the world indicates that whether governments classify themselves as socialist, Marxist-Leninist, or capitalist, they choose policy objectives and policy instruments that span a very wide range of alternatives. And policies can be similar for governments that profess to hold quite different philosophies.

Nonetheless, it is clear that many leaders in the antiapartheid movement would not find the particular configuration of policy choices suggested above congenial. Many now engaged in the struggle would seek a stronger commitment to social ownership of the means of production, a clearer argument for redistribution of income, and a commitment to higher wages for all black labor.

It is important for the major antiapartheid organizations to think in concrete terms about the nature of the economic policies they might pursue in a postapartheid society. With only general statements of intention available, the forces opposed to change have the ability (which they have used) to paint those statements in the worst possible light for their own purposes with their own constituents. This situation inhibits the movement toward discussion and negotiation about a sensible transfer of power—and this, in turn, gives ammunition to opponents of fundamental change. The antiapartheid movement itself would also benefit from a thorough discussion of economic alternatives after apartheid. While the primary focus of the movement now must be on the political struggle, there are interactions between the vision of the future and the nature of the process by which that vision is realized.

ALTERNATIVE TRANSITIONS

The discussion of options available to a postapartheid government has been based on the assumption that a transition could come rapidly and with a minimum of additional bloodshed and economic disruption, but has not attempted to place a precise definition on either the speed or the peacefulness of the process. Even if the transition were speedily accomplished, the new government would face a wide range of difficult problems as it tried to dismantle the effects of a century of separation and discrimination, and to build a new society and economy. Unfortunately, a quick and easy transition looks distressingly unlikely, and the problems facing a postapartheid government will therefore be considerably different from those suggested here, and a good deal more difficult to handle.

Consider only two prospects. Suppose that the level of violence and repression increases, that the government does make some adjustments to an alternative development strategy along with its reformist approach to politics, and that the international community increases the level of economic sanctions applied to

South Africa. These conditions will eventually lead to a winding down of the economy, growing black and eventually white unemployment, and a general depletion of the capital stock. The situation might approximate Zimbabwe's at independence. The new government there benefited from an improvement in the terms of trade because of the lifting of sanctions, but capital stock, both public and private, was considerably depreciated, and the years prior to and immediately after independence saw the departure of a number of skilled whites, though an inflow of former exiles also followed independence. Even with serious economic disruption, Zimbabwe was able to make a relatively quick transition. Initial growth in the domestic economy was rapid; capital, including concessional finance, flowed in from abroad; some land resettlement provided immediate satisfaction for blacks, as well as additional income opportunities and agricultural output; and the private sector in mining, manufacturing, and agriculture performed quite well under a new government. Major problems remain—some of them due to the survival of apartheid in South Africa. A number of macroeconomic issues—particularly regarding budgetary control, exchange rate and exchange control policies, and wages—might have been handled in a way that was more conducive to better and more sustained overall economic performance so as to give the country and the government more resources to work with. Nonetheless, the transition in Zimbabwe, after a bitter civil war, was accomplished with considerable success in political, social, and economic terms. South Africa, of course, has a larger white population and a more sophisticated, urbanized economy. But Zimbabwe's experience suggests that a transition in South Africa, even if it took place after a relatively long armed struggle, could result in the promise of real and rapid improvement in economic conditions for all.

If, however, South Africa moves in a direction where the maintenance of white control, regardless of the cost, becomes paramount, then the prospects for the postapartheid government are a good deal more grim. Those conditions will necessarily cause disruption of major sectors of the economy, destruction of large parts of the basic infrastructure, and relocation of much of the population. Emigration is likely to be high, leaving the government with a shattered economy and a labor force that has been depleted of skilled and educated people. A transition that follows such a period will take place against a background of even higher levels of hate and mistrust than currently exist. There will be major problems in repairing not just the economy but the society and polity as well. In this scenario, it is all too easy to see the intransigence of large portions of the white population, combined with the frustration and desperation of blacks, producing a tragic outcome.

A SUMMING UP

Since the discovery of diamonds and gold in the late 1800s, economic development in South Africa has been shaped by two factors: the country's tremendous mineral wealth and the government's policy of systematic, legally enforced racial discrimination known as apartheid. For most of the twentieth century, South Africa's economy grew rapidly by international standards. In the early 1970s, however, economic growth began to slow; by the 1980s it had ground to a virtual halt. Had South Africa been able to achieve the same rate of growth from 1975 to 1987 that it had experienced from 1946 to 1975, the country's economy would have been roughly 45 percent larger (see Figure 6.1). The bulk of this difference can be attributed to the diseconomies of the apartheid system and the costs of preserving white rule.

Apartheid is, quite simply, inconsistent with long-term economic growth. Sustained economic development requires, and produces, an increasingly integrated, interdependent economy; apartheid by definition prevents integration and interdependence. To enhance and preserve white welfare and security, South Africa's rulers have restricted black access to land, education, training, and credit; limited the movement of workers and their families; created economically nonviable black homelands; established large and costly bureaucracies; and invested large sums in noneconomic projects. As a consequence, the overall productivity of investment in South Africa has declined dramatically since the mid-1960s.

The burdens of apartheid have been greatly increased by the steadily rising costs of preserving white rule in the face of mounting external pressure. By reducing trade and investment flows and forcing investment in uneconomical projects, international pressure has imposed substantial costs on the country. By some estimates these costs could be as high as $2 billion a year.

It is not entirely clear how the economic costs of apartheid and international pressure have affected the nature and pace of political change in South Africa. It is clear, however, that economic pressures have played a major role in forcing the South African government to change its policies on a wide range of issues from labor reform to the release of political prisoners; and that in the absence of fundamental political change, the prospects for economic growth in South Africa are bleak.

The long and bitter debate over the legitimacy of using economic sanctions to promote political change in South Africa is now largely over. In testimony before the U.S. Congress in October 1989, Assistant Secretary of State for Africa Herman Cohen officially acknowledged that economic sanctions had played a positive role in changing white attitudes. What remains to be decided is how additional sanctions—or the relaxation of existing sanctions—can be used to speed up the process of change. Whatever steps are taken, however, their impact will depend in large part on the extent to which they are supported by a coalition including all of South Africa's major economic partners. The most effective program would involve concerted multilateral pressure from all of the major industrial powers.

Once the need for fundamental change is recognized, economic progress could be a handmaiden of political progress. Removing the costs of maintaining white rule and freeing the economy of apartheid's restrictions could produce a substantial period of high growth. High growth would ease the transition to a postapartheid society that would address the needs and the rightful claims of the black majority while minimizing the economic losses for large numbers of whites. It would also reduce substantially potential conflicts that might arise over economic issues. The quicker the transition to a postapartheid society, the greater would be the potential economic gains.

In order for growth to play such a role, however, *either* a postapartheid government would have to be in place *or* the black majority would have to be convinced that fundamental political changes were actually being made. Because people's views of the future affect their actions, I believe that an explicit discussion of the postapartheid economy and its considerable promise could be a positive element in fostering negotiations among the various parties on the abolition of white rule and the transition to a nonracial society. And the sooner that happens, the better will be the lives of more than 100 million people throughout southern Africa.

NOTES

INTRODUCTION

1. This argument is often associated with Michael O'Dowd, of the Anglo American Corporation, and others in the business community in South Africa and abroad.
2. For an extensive treatment of this subject, see, in particular, Merle Lipton, *Capitalism and Apartheid: South Africa, 1910–1986* (Aldershot: Wildwood House, 1986).
3. This address, "The Anatomy of Segregation," is reprinted in C. Cooper et al., *Race Relations 1985* (Johannesburg: South African Institute of Race Relations, 1986), the fiftieth anniversary of the institute's invaluable annual survey.
4. Commonwealth Group of Eminent Persons, *Mission to South Africa: The Commonwealth Report* (Harmondsworth, Middlesex: Penguin, 1986), 41.
5. Ibid., 42.

1: THE ORIGINS OF THE APARTHEID ECONOMY

1. D. Hobart Houghton, *The South African Economy*, 4th ed. (Cape Town: Oxford University Press, 1976).
2. These acts made it a criminal offense for an employer or employee to breach an employment contract. In practice, however, the courts had made them applicable principally to unskilled workers, mainly blacks, not their employers. Other such actions include Transvaal Ordinance No. 17 of 1904, which limited employment of non-European immigrants to unskilled labor, and the establishment of minimum ratios of white to non-white mine workers in response to a strike in 1907.
3. During the Rand Rebellion the South African Communist Party flew its banner proclaiming: "Workers of the World Unite and Fight for a White South Africa."

2: GROWTH AND STRUCTURE OF SOUTH AFRICA'S ECONOMY

1. Michael D. McGrath, *Inequality in the Size Distribution of Incomes in South Africa*, Staff Paper, no. 2 (Durban: Development Studies Unit, University of Natal, 1984).
2. In 1963 over 16,000 immigrants who had been born in Kenya, South

Africa, Rhodesia, and Zambia went to South Africa; in 1964 the number was over 12,000. Beginning in 1973 net immigration began from Rhodesia, and from 1973 through 1979 over 45,000 people migrated to South Africa, while just over 6,500 moved in the other direction. The flow to South Africa rose every year from 1972 through 1980.

3. Hollis B. Chenery et al., *Redistribution with Growth* (London: Oxford University Press, 1974).

4. These figures are derived from data in South African Reserve Bank, *Quarterly Bulletin*, March 1988, and updated by data from International Monetary Fund, *Industrial Financial Statistics* (Washington, D.C., 1989).

5. Development Bank of Southern Africa, *Annual Report 1985–86*.

6. See S. Herbert Frankel, *Capital Investment in Africa: Its course and effects* (London: Oxford University Press, 1958); and D. Hobart Houghton, *The South African Economy*, 11.

7. Adjustment in a "soft" employment situation may be illustrated by the fact that between 1983 and 1984 the number of blacks employed by the central government, local authorities, and the Department of Posts and Telecommunications fell, as did total employment in all those categories, while the number of whites in each case rose.

8. For a careful analysis based on firm-level data, see J. B. Kright and M. D. McGrath, "An Analysis of Racial Wage Discrimination in South Africa," *Oxford Bulletin of Economics and Statistics* 39, no. 4 (1987): 245–27. The authors point out how formal methods of job evaluation for setting relative pay scales that were introduced in the mid-1970s undermined the practice of setting wage rates based on the racial composition of the people currently doing the job, and they note that nine of ten multinationals and half of local companies reported using formal job evaluations in 1982.

9. Of nearly 5.8 million black pupils, only 151,107 were in schools that had adopted compulsory education in 1984, in part because the school committees must request that it be introduced. No compulsory education existed in any of the homelands. Compulsory education exists for whites and coloreds to age sixteen, and for Asians to age fifteen. See the chapter on education in C. Cooper et al., *Race Relations*.

10. The figures on income distribution are drawn from many sources and use a variety of definitions. Generally, they do not take account of income taxes or of the distribution of benefits received from government expenditures. Conventional wisdom in the South African business community has it that, in view of the progressive nature of the income tax, whites pay higher taxes than blacks, and post-tax inequalities are thus less. The conventional wisdom seems suspect, since a number of questions are unclear: the impact of such regressive taxes as the general sales tax, the effect of tariffs, whether the underlying estimates include noncash income, whether taxes are shifted through price increases and other mechanisms from whites to blacks, and who can be said to benefit from the various expenditures of the state (including the large security expenditures).

11. Michael D. McGrath, *Inequality in the Size Distribution of Incomes in South Africa*.

12. Among the many descriptions of commuter life for Africans, that of Joseph Lelyveld in *Move Your Shadow* (Harmondsworth, Middlesex: Penguin, 1985) is outstanding for its combination of the human element and a quantification of the costs to individuals, families, and the society at large.

13. For a discussion of the various estimates that have been made, see C. Cooper et al., *Race Relations*, 437–88. The Surplus People Project estimated that 3.5 million people of all races were removed between 1960 and 1982. The minister of cooperation and development at the time disputed the figure and said the correct number was 1.99 million.

14. Data on the growth of government employment tell a similar story. For the total of all homelands, black government employment increased by 13 percent annually for 1973 to 1978, while the six "nonindependent" homelands had 7 percent yearly increases in black government employment from 1978 to 1982.

15. Since blacks own land in white areas only on sufferance, if at all, one could look at per capita arable land on the basis of race rather than residence. In 1985 whites had access to 2.54 arable hectares per capita, while blacks had 0.08. Data on arable land and 1985 agricultural GDP are from Michael Cobbett, "Agriculture in South Africa's Homelands," paper presented at York University, York, UK, 1986.

16. Ibid. Cobbett cites evidence suggesting that more than 40 percent of homeland residents were not living in rural areas even within the homelands.

17. Department of Foreign Affairs, *South African Manual: The Promotion of Industrial Development as an Element of a Co-ordinated Regional Development Strategy for Southern Africa* (Pretoria: Government Printer, 1982). The manual provides figures for all regions. A decentralization board was established in 1982 to administer the schemes.

18. As one would expect in a large subsidy program, there are abuses. One report cited two firms in the Ciskei that reported employing 520 cleaners, 326 security guards, and 128 gardeners, all of whom were to qualify for the R110-per-month wage subsidy from the program.

19. In general, any form of protection means that incomes paid will exceed incomes earned in saving or earning foreign currency, and South Africa has relatively generous protection levels. If, in addition to the normal protection, enterprises are paid the levels of subsidy inherent in the decentralization incentives, the subsidies themselves can result in income payments when no *real* value added occurs. When profits are owned by foreigners and leave the country, the subsidies go outside the country and can easily exceed the value of the capital brought in. This situation is exacerbated when the financial rand is used, as discussed in chapter 3. From 1982–1983 to 1984–1985 over 150 foreign projects, representing investments totaling R300 million, were approved.

20. These data, from C. Cooper et al., *Race Relations,* are based on the reports of the minister of manpower.

21. Of the many analyses of apartheid's overall effects, its effects on different interest groups, and, particularly, its relationship to capitalism, among the

most thorough and persuasive appears in Merle Lipton, *Capitalism and Apartheid*. Much of the discussion here follows that detailed analysis.

3: SOUTH AFRICA AND THE INTERNATIONAL ECONOMY

1. These comparisons are based on data from World Bank, *World Development Report* (Washington, D.C., 1986).
2. A variety of estimates have been made of the premium South Africa pays for its oil. In a 1986 speech, President P. W. Botha put the total cost at R22 billion, which probably includes the capital costs of SASOL and the cost of stockpiling oil. Other estimates place the premium at around $2 billion per year, with the exact amount varying according to the state of world oil markets and the level of imports. The latter figure would be very high for recent international markets. South Africa has stockpiled considerable oil, so the total import bill and the total premium in the past decade have been larger than would be required to run an economy that was not stockpiling.
3. S. Herbert Frankel, *Capital Investment in Africa*.
4. Historical figures are given in Merle Lipton, *Capitalism and Apartheid*. *South African Statistics* carried a series on the share of mining dividends paid abroad until its 1970 issue. The most recent figure was for 1968, when 25 percent were paid abroad.
5. If an investment yielded a 15 percent return in rand terms, and one could buy the capital at a 50 percent discount through the financial rand, one's investment in foreign currency terms would yield 30 percent. Alternatively put, in order to attract foreign capital, South Africa would be offering a return to foreigners of twice that available to domestic investors.

4: SOUTH AFRICA AND THE REGION

1. The tables and the general argument presented here are taken from Steven Lewis, "Some Economic Realities in Southern Africa: One Hundred Million Futures," in Coralie Bryant, ed., *Poverty, Policy, and Food Security in Southern Africa* (Boulder: Lynne Rienner Publishers Inc., 1988).
2. Some figures show that Botswana imports a substantial portion of its electricity from South Africa. It did so on an interim basis during construction of the national grid distributing power from a central coal-fired power station in central Botswana, but now uses South African power principally on a standby basis.
3. E.L. McFarland, Jr., "The Benefits to RSA of Her Exports to the BLS Countries," *Botswana's Economy since Independence* (New Dehli, Tatta: McGraw Hill, 1983).
4. Much of the growth in Lesotho was driven by the increase in migrant workers' earnings from mining employment in South Africa, a response to the rapid increases in real mine worker pay in the 1970s.
5. Because the Botswana-Zimbabwe agreement predated the renegotiation

of the Southern African Customs Union agreement, the parties to the latter accepted the provisions of the former. Reexport of Zimbabwean goods to South Africa from Botswana is prohibited, of course.

5: EXTERNAL ECONOMIC PRESSURES AND SOUTH AFRICAN REACTIONS

1. The Cuban presence in Angola suggests that the equation cannot be limited to the countries of the region alone.
2. A detailed review is contained in a May 1987 report to Congress (mandated by the Comprehensive Anti-Apartheid Act of 1986); Merle Lipton, *Capitalism and Apartheid;* and Joseph Hanlon and Roger Omond, *The Sanctions Handbook* (Harmondsworth, Middlesex: Penguin, 1987).
3. J.P. Hayes, *Economic Effects of Sanctions on Southern Africa* (London: Trade Policy Research Centre, 1987); and *The Effect of Sanctions on Employment and Production in South Africa: A Quantitative Analysis* (The Federated Chamber of Industries, 1986).
4. While the DeBeers' Central Selling Organization (CSO) is under control of South African companies, a declining share (now around 20 percent) of total CSO sales is accounted for by diamonds mined in South Africa. Official export trade statistics from South Africa include diamonds mined in Botswana and Namibia (and very small amounts in Lesotho and Swaziland). While experts differ, it is generally believed that rough diamonds can be identified by the mine of origin, which would in principle make it possible to impose sanctions against South African diamonds without interfering with prices of diamonds from other countries. Advocates of the practice argue that the CSO—which markets on behalf of producers in countries as diverse as Australia, the Soviet Union, Botswana, and Tanzania—would be willing to eliminate South African diamonds from its sales in exchange for exemption from sanctions. My own view, based on some contact with the diamond trade over the past decade, is that even with CSO agreement, the enforcement machinery (including the need to litigate over the origin of specific parcels of rough diamonds) would be very cumbersome; furthermore, given other aspects of secrecy in the diamond trade, as well as its high profitability, the potential for leakages would be great indeed. Hence my skepticism about imposing effective sanctions on South African diamonds.
5. J.P. Hayes, *Economic Effects of Sanctions on Southern Africa.*

6: APARTHEID, ECONOMICS, AND POLITICAL CHANGE

1. The ratios for the decades ending in 1986 and 1987 are so high that they are not graphed in Figure 6.2. Using averages of coefficients calculated over a five-year period helps smooth annual variations, but the disastrous

results of the early 1980s, in which use of installed capacity in industries declined substantially, are almost certainly temporary.
2. The declining capital requirements from the late 1940s through the mid-1960s may reflect in part the savings noted earlier from not having to provide urban infrastructure, housing, and services to migrant laborers.

7: A POSTAPARTHEID ECONOMY

1. South Africa has neglected the small-scale sector for decades. S. Herbert Frankel, *Capital Investment in Africa,* 127, notes that from 1910 to 1937 the South African government spent over £112 million on agriculture, of which "the amount made available directly for native agricultural needs was less than £750,000." It will take a major investment in new research and extension to deal effectively with any initiative for small-scale agriculture for black South Africans.
2. Such an exchange rate policy, of course, raises the profitability of primary exports as well; but given that the rate of tax on gold mines depends on the ratio of profits to total income, the government would receive a rising share of increased profits that resulted from this kind of policy. An aggressive exchange rate policy might call for a review of other tax regimes on primary exports.

APPENDIX

TABLE A. INTERNATIONAL MIGRATION, 1947–1984

Period	Immigration	Emigration	Net immigration
		Total migration	
1947–1948	66,561	15,663	50,898
1949–1962	219,092	163,637	55,455
1963–1976	553,001	132,174	420,827
1977–1979	62,171	62,380	−209
1980–1984	176,455	42,692	133,763
1985–1987	31,378	34,412	−3,034
Total	*1,108,658*	*450,958*	*657,700*
		Annual average	
1947–1948	33,281	7,832	25,449
1949–1962	15,649	11,688	3,961
1963–1976	39,500	9,441	30,059
1977–1979	20,724	20,793	−70
1980–1984	35,291	8,538	26,753
1985–1987	10,459	11,471	−1,011
Total	*27,040*	*10,999*	*16,041*

Source: Republic of South Africa, *Bulletin of Statistics,* various issues.

TABLE B. AVERAGE GROSS DOMESTIC INVESTMENT AND SAVING AS PERCENTAGES OF GDP, 1947–1986*

Period	Investment	Saving
1947–1951	26.50	17.23
1952–1956	24.90	21.76
1957–1961	23.40	24.49
1962–1966	24.82	24.35
1967–1971	29.38	25.40
1972–1976	30.69	27.08
1977–1981	28.51	30.70
1982–1986	23.57	24.63

Sources: South African Reserve Bank, *Quarterly Bulletin,* various issues.

* Percentages are at current prices; GDP is at factor cost.

175

TABLE C. RELATIVE WAGES IN SOUTH AFRICAN GOLD MINES,
1911–1985

Year	Real earnings in 1985 prices		Current rand		White/ African ratio	Index of real earnings	
	White	African	White	African		White	African
1911	13,327	1,128	666	57	11.7:1	102	100
1916	12,282	1,015	709	59	12.0:1	94	90
1921	11,759	778	992	66	15.0:1	90	69
1926	11,106	993	753	67	11.2:1	85	88
1931	11,759	1,038	753	66	11.3:1	90	92
1936	13,066	1,128	786	68	11.5:1	100	100
1941	12,282	1,004	848	70	12.1:1	94	89
1946	12,935	1,038	1,106	87	12.7:1	99	92
1951	14,765	1,004	1,607	109	14.7:1	113	89
1956	15,548	1,004	2,046	132	15.5:1	119	89
1961	16,855	1,004	2,478	146	17.0:1	129	89
1966	19,468	1,117	3,216	183	17.6:1	149	99
1970	24,172	1,207	4,545	227	20.0:1	185	107
1975	26,001	3,023	7,629	889	8.6:1	199	268
1980	23,911	3,982	12,419	2,068	6.0:1	183	353
1985	24,564	4,320	24,564	4,320	5.7:1	188	383

Sources: For 1911–1966, Francis Wilson, *Labour in the South African Gold Mines 1911–1969* (London: Cambridge University Press, 1972), 66. For 1970–1980, Republic of South Africa, *South African Statistics*, 1982. For 1985, C. Cooper et al., *Race Relations, 1985* (Johannesburg: South African Institute of Race Relations, 1986).

TABLE D. WAGE RATIO, WHITE TO OTHER RACES, BY SECTOR,
1960–1985

Year	Colored	Asian	African
	Mining and quarrying		
1960	4.7:1	3.5:1	15.8:1
1965	5.2:1	4.1:1	16.6:1
1970	5.1:1	3.9:1	19.8:1
1975	4.0:1	3.1:1	8.6:1
1980	3.3:1	2.4:1	6.0:1
1985	3.2:1	2.0:1	5.7:1
	Manufacturing		
1960	3.4:1	3.2:1	5.4:1
1965	3.7:1	3.6:1	5.1:1
1970	4.2:1	3.9:1	5.8:1
1975	3.8:1	3.4:1	4.8:1
1980	3.6:1	3.2:1	4.3:1
1985	3.5:1	2.8:1	3.9:1

TABLE D. CONTINUED

Year	Colored	Asian	African
		Construction	
1960	2.7 : 1	2.5 : 1	5.7 : 1
1965	2.3 : 1	2.2 : 1	5.4 : 1
1970	3.0 : 1	2.3 : 1	6.5 : 1
1975	2.6 : 1	2.0 : 1	4.9 : 1
1980	3.4 : 1	2.1 : 1	5.3 : 1
1985	3.0 : 1	1.7 : 1	4.7 : 1
		Central government	
1960	3.0 : 1	2.0 : 1	4.5 : 1
1965	1.7 : 1	1.7 : 1	4.7 : 1
1970	2.4 : 1	1.9 : 1	6.1 : 1
1975	2.3 : 1	1.4 : 1	4.1 : 1
1980	2.3 : 1	1.2 : 1	3.1 : 1
1985	1.8 : 1	1.1 : 1	2.5 : 1
		All sectors	
1970	3.5 : 1	3.1 : 1	6.8 : 1
1975	3.1 : 1	2.6 : 1	4.9 : 1
1980	3.1 : 1	2.4 : 1	4.1 : 1
1985	2.8 : 1	2.0 : 1	3.8 : 1

Sources: Calculated from employment and earnings data in Republic of South Africa, *South African Statistics,* 1976 and 1982, and Republic of South Africa, *Bulletin of Statistics,* December 1986.

TABLE E. GOLD EXPORTS AS PERCENTAGE OF GDP AND OF VISIBLE EXPORTS, 1912–1985*

Period*	GDP	Exports
1912	24.4	61.6
1920	12.7	40.6
1925	12.8	41.3
1930	13.4	50.0
1935	12.5	58.0
1940	23.9	73.1
1945	13.9	57.7
1951–1955	9.5	32.3
1956–1960	10.2	35.8
1961–1965	10.7	48.4
1966–1970	7.8	35.6
1971–1975	9.3	39.7

TABLE E. CONTINUED

Period*	GDP	Exports
1976-1980	11.8	37.7
1981-1985	11.6	46.5

Sources: For 1912–1945, calculated from D. Hobart Houghton, *The South African Economy,* 4th ed. (Cape Town: Oxford University Press, 1976); and Republic of South Africa, *South African Statistics,* 1976. For 1946–1985, calculated from South African Reserve Bank, *Quarterly Bulletin,* various issues.

* Five-year average.

TABLE F. NET FOREIGN CAPITAL INFLOW AS PERCENTAGE OF GDP AND OF GROSS DOMESTIC INVESTMENT, 1946–1987*

Period*	GDP	Investment
1946-1950	8.9	31.7
1951-1955	4.3	13.1
1956-1960	-0.5	-1.3
1961-1965	-0.4	-1.0
1966-1970	3.1	12.4
1971-1975	4.1	15.5
1976-1980	-2.3	-6.2
1981-1985	1.0	4.4
1983-1987	-2.7	-12.8

Source: South African Reserve Bank, national accounts tables.

* Five-year average.

TABLE G. PERCENTAGE DISTRIBUTION OF LIABILITIES TO FOREIGNERS BY TYPE, AND TOTAL FOREIGN INVESTMENT, 1956–1985

	Percentage distribution				Total investment (billions of U.S. $)
	Long-term investment				
Year	Private direct	Other private*	Public sector†	Short-term investment††	
1956	47.1	28.8	8.2	15.8	3.87
1965	54.5	16.1	9.2	20.2	4.86
1970	55.2	16.9	8.3	19.6	8.15
1975	36.0	17.3	24.2	22.5	18.93
1980	41.7	18.4	21.2	18.7	34.19
1981	37.3	16.0	19.4	27.3	33.97
1982	33.3	14.5	21.1	31.0	37.04

TABLE G. CONTINUED

	Percentage distribution				Total investment (billions of U.S. $)
	Long-term investment				
Year	Private direct	Other private*	Public sector†	Short-term investment††	
1983	30.8	13.9	21.3	34.1	37.64
1984	24.8	13.0	20.9	41.4	33.75
1985	22.3	13.0	21.9	42.7	31.84

Sources: South African Reserve Bank, Quarterly Bulletin, various issues, tables on foreign liabilities, converted to dollars at year-end exchange rates.

* Includes both equity and debt.
† Includes both public authorities and parastatal corporations.
†† Includes both public- and private-sector liabilities due for payment within one year.

TABLE H. UNDISTRIBUTED PROFITS AS PERCENTAGE OF TOTAL BOOK VALUE OF DIRECT FOREIGN INVESTMENT, 1956–1985*

Period*	Investment
1956–1960	60.4
1961–1965	65.0
1966–1970	70.2
1971–1975	78.4
1976–1980	82.6
1981–1985	86.0

Sources: For 1956–1978, Republic of South Africa, South African Statistics, various issues. For 1979–1985, South African Reserve Bank, Quarterly Bulletin, various issues, tables on foreign assets and liabilities.

Note: Percentages were calculated by dividing share premium, reserves, and undistributed profits by the sum of the nominal value of ordinary and other shares plus share premium, reserves, and undistributed profits.

* Five-year average.

SUGGESTED READINGS

Bailey, Martin and Bernard Rivers. "Oil Sanctions Against South Africa." UN Centre Against Apartheid, No. 15/80. New York, April 1980.

Barber, James P.; Jesmond Blumenfeld; and Christopher R. Hill. *The West and South Africa*. London: Royal Institute of International Affairs; Boston: Routledge & Kegan Paul, 1982.

Bissell, Richard E. *South Africa and the United States: The Erosion of an Influence Relationship*. New York: Praeger, 1982.

Black, P.A. and B.E. Dollery. "Martin Legassick's Postscript to Legislation, Ideology and Economy in Post-1948 South Africa: A Critical Note." *South African Journal of Economics* 47, no. 3 (September 1979).

Blumenfeld, Jesmond, ed. *South Africa in Crisis*. London: Royal Institute of International Affairs, Croom Helm, 1987.

Botha, D.J.J. "An Economic Boycott of South Africa?" (review article). *South African Journal of Economics* 46, no. 3 (September 1978).

Brown, F.D. "Amandla! The Rallying Cry Against Apartheid." *Black Enterprise* 15 (April 1985).

Chamber of Mines of South Africa. *Ninety-fifth Annual Report 1984*. Johannesburg, 1985.

Clifford-Vaughn, F. McA. *International Pressures and Political Change in South Africa*. Cape Town and New York: Oxford University Press, 1978.

Cobbe, J.H. "Growth and Change in Lesotho" (review article). *South African Journal of Economics* 46, no. 2 (June 1978).

Coetzee, J.M. *Life and Times of Michael K*. New York: Penguin, 1985.

Commonwealth Group of Eminent Persons. *Mission to South Africa: The Commonwealth Report*. New York: Penguin, 1986.

Council on Economic Priorities. *Pension Funds and Ethical Investment: A Study of Investment Practices and Opportunities*. New York: State of

California Retirement Systems, Council on Economic Priorities, 1980.

Croizat, Victor J. *The Economic Development of South Africa in its Political Context.* Santa Monica, California: Rand Corporation, 1967.

Daniel, Philip, ed. "Mineral Exporters in Boom and Slump." *IDS Bulletin* 17, no. 4 (October 1986).

Davids, C.W. *The Impact of Economic Sanctions Against South Africa on the SADCC States.* Ottawa: Canadian International Development Agency, February 1986.

Davies, Robert H. *The Struggle for South Africa: A Reference Guide to Movements, Organizations, and Institutions.* London: Zed Books, 1984.

Davis, Jennifer; James Cason; and Gail Hovey. "Economic Disengagement and South Africa: The Effectiveness and Feasibility of Implementing Sanctions and Divestment." *Law and Policy in International Business* 15, no. 2 (1983).

Denoon, Donald. *Settler Capitalism: The Dynamics of Dependent Development in the Southern Hemisphere.* Oxford: Clarendon Press, 1983.

Development Bank of Southern Africa. *Annual Report.* 1985–86.

DuPlessis, J.C. "Foreign Investment in South Africa." In I. Livtak and C. Maule, eds., *Foreign Investment: The Experience of Host Countries.* New York: Praeger, 1970.

Ettinger, Stephen Joel. "The Economics of the Customs Union Between Botswana, Lesotho, Swaziland and South Africa." Thesis, University of Michigan, 1974.

First, Ruth; Jonathan Steele; and Christabel Gurney. *The South African Connection: Western Investment in Apartheid.* New York: Barnes & Noble, 1973.

Frankel, S. Herbert. *Capital Investment in Africa: Its Course and Effects.* London: Oxford University Press, 1958.

Freer, P.A. and D. Samson. *South Africa: Business Prospects Re-Assessed.* Special Report No. 126. London: Economist Intelligence Unit, 1982.

Geldenhuys, Deon. *The Diplomacy of Isolation: South African Foreign Policy Making.* New York: St. Martin's Press, 1984.

Green, Reginald Herbold; Dereje Asrat; Marta Mauras; and Richard Morgan. *Children in Southern Africa.* Report prepared for UNICEF. New York, March 1987.

Gregory, Theodor E.G. *Ernest Oppenheimer and the Economic Development of Southern Africa.* New York: Arno Press, 1977.

Hance, William A., ed. *Southern Africa and the United States*. New York: Columbia University Press, 1968.

Hanlon, Joseph. *SADCC: Progress, Projects and Prospects*. Special Report No. 182. London: Economist Intelligence Unit, 1984.

Hanlon, Joseph and Roger Omond. *The Sanctions Handbook*. Harmondsworth: Penguin, 1987.

Hauck, David. *Two Decades of Debate: The Controversy Over U.S. Companies in South Africa*. Washington, D.C.: Investor Responsibility Research Center, 1983.

Hauck, David. *U.S. Corporate Withdrawal from South Africa: The Likely Impact on Political Change*. Washington, D.C.: Investor Responsibility Research Center, 1986.

Hero, Alfred O., Jr. and John Barret, eds. *The American People and South Africa: Publics, Elites and Policymaking*. Lexington, MA: Lexington Books, 1981.

Hill, Christopher R. *Changes in South Africa: Blind Alleys or New Directions?* Ottawa and New Jersey: Barnes & Noble, 1983.

Horrell, Muriel. *The African Homelands of South Africa*. Johannesburg: South Africa Institute of Race Relations, June 1973.

Horwitz, Ralph. *The Political Economy of South Africa*. New York: Praeger, 1967.

Hough, M.; W. Booyse; and M. Van Der Merwe. *Selected South and Southern African Treaties, Agreements and Declarations*. Pretoria: Institute for Strategic Studies, 1985.

Houghton, D. Hobart. *The South African Economy*, 4th ed. Cape Town and New York: Oxford University Press, 1976.

Houghton, D. Hobart and Jennifer Dagut. *Source Material on the South African Economy*. Cape Town and New York: Oxford University Press, 1972.

Jaster, Robert S. *A Regional Security Role for Africa's Front-Line States: Experience and Prospects*. London: International Institute for Strategic Studies, 1983.

Jaster, Robert S. "South Africa and its Neighbours: The Dynamics of Regional Conflict." IISS *Adelphi Papers* 209 (1986).

Johnson, Richard William. *How Long will South Africa Survive?* New York: Oxford University Press, 1977.

Kiewiet, Cornelis Willemde. *A History of South Africa, Social and Economic*. Oxford: The Clarendon Press, 1941.

Knight, J.B. "Labour Allocation and Unemployment in South Africa." *Oxford Bulletin of Economic Statistics* 40, no. 2 (May 1978).

Knight, J.B. "The Nature of Unemployment in South Africa." *The South African Journal of Economics* 50, no. 1 (1982).

Knight, J.B. and G. Lenta. "Has Capitalism Underdeveloped the Labour Reserves of South Africa?" *Oxford Bulletin of Economic Statistics* 42, no. 3 (August 1980).

Knight, J.B. and M.D. McGrath. "An Analysis of Racial Wage Discrimination in South Africa." *Oxford Bulletin of Economics and Statistics* 39, no. 4 (November 1977).

Kock, Michiel Hendrik D. *The Economic Development of South Africa.* London: P.S. King & Son, Ltd., 1936.

Landell-Mills, Pierre. "The Southern African Customs Union: A Comment on Mosley's Reappraisal." *World Development* 7, no. 1 (January 1979).

Leape, Jonathan; Bo Baskin; and Stefan Underhill, eds. *Business in the Shadow of Apartheid: U.S. Firms in South Africa.* Lexington, MA: Lexington Books, 1985.

Leiss, Amelia Catherine, ed. *Apartheid and UN Collective Measures, an Analysis.* New York: Carnegie Endowment for International Peace, 1965.

Lelyveld, Joseph. *Move Your Shadow.* Harmondsworth: Penguin, 1985.

Lewis, Jon. *Industrialization and Trade Union Organizations in South Africa 1924–55.* New York: Cambridge University Press, 1984.

Liff, David M. *The Oil Industry in South Africa.* Washington, D.C.: Investor Responsibility Research Center, January 1979.

Lipton, Merle. *Capitalism and Apartheid: South Africa, 1910–1986.* Aldershot: Wildwood House Ltd., 1986.

Livtak, Lawrence; Robert DeGrasse; and Kathleen McTigue. *South Africa, Foreign Investment and Apartheid.* Washington, D.C.: Institute for Policy Studies, 1978.

Lundahl, Mats. "The Rationale of Apartheid." *American Economic Review* 72 (December 1982).

Maasdorp, Gavin. "The Southern African Customs Union—An Assessment." *Journal of Contemporary African Studies* 2, no. 1 (October 1982).

Macmillan, Hugh. *Economists, Apartheid and "The Common Society."* York: Centre for Southern African Studies, 1986.

Macmillan, William Miller. *Complex South Africa: An Economic Foot-note to History.* London: Faber & Faber Limited, 1930.

Magubane, Bernard. *The Political Economy of Race and Class in South Africa.* New York: Monthly Review Press, 1979.

Malan, T. "Economic Sanctions as Policy Instrument to Effect Change—The Case of South Africa." *Finance and Trade Review* xiv, no. 3 (June 1981).

Malan, T. and P.S. Hattingh. *Black Homelands in South Africa.* Pretoria: Africa Institute of South Africa, 1976.

Marcelle, Kooy, ed. *Studies in Economics and Economic History: Essays in Honour of Professor H.M. Robertson.* Durham, NC: Duke University Press, 1972.

Mbeki, Govan. *South Africa: The Peasants' Revolt.* London: International Defence and Aid Fund for Southern Africa, 1984.

McGrath, Michael. *Inequality in the Size Distribution of Incomes in South Africa,* Staff Paper No. 2. Durban: Development Studies Unit, University of Natal, 1984.

Minter, William. *King Solomon's Mines Revisited: Western Interests and the Burdened History of Southern Africa.* New York: Basic Books, 1986.

Moorsom, Richard. *The Scope for Sanctions: Economic Measures Against South Africa.* London: Catholic Institute for International Relations, 1986.

Murray, Martin. *South African Capitalism and Black Political Opposition.* Cambridge, MA: Schenkman Publishing Company, 1982.

Myers, Desaix B. *Labor Practices of U.S. Corporations in South Africa.* New York: Praeger, 1977.

Myers, Desaix B. *U.S. Business in South Africa: The Economic, Political and Moral Issues.* Bloomington: Indiana University Press, 1980.

Nattrass, Jill. *The South African Economy: Its Growth and Change.* Cape Town: Oxford University Press, 1981.

Newman, Anne and Cathy Bowers. *Foreign Investment in South Africa and Namibia: A Directory of U.S., Canadian, and British Companies Operating in South Africa and Namibia; With a Survey of the 100 Largest U.S. Bank Holding Companies and Their Practices and Policies on Lending to South Africa.* Washington, D.C.: Investor Responsibility Research Center, 1984.

Nielsen, J. "Time to Quit South Africa?" *Fortune* 112 (September 30, 1980).

Palmer, G.F. "South Africa." (Address, May 13, 1980.) *Vital Speeches* 46 (June 15, 1980).

Paton, Alan. *Cry, the Beloved Country.* New York: Scribners, 1948.

Porter, Richard C. "Apartheid, the Job Ladder, and the Evolutionary Hypothesis: Empirical Evidence from South African Manufacturing, 1960–1977." *Economics of Development and Cultural Change* 33 (1984).

Porter, Richard C. "International Trade and Investment Sanctions. Potential Impact on the South African Economy." *Journal of Conflict Resolution* 23 (December 1979).

Porter, Richard C. "A Model of the South African–type Economy." *American Economic Review* 68 (December 1978).

Republic of South Africa. *Official Yearbook of the Republic of South Africa.* 1974, 1980/81, and 1985.

Republic of South Africa. *Statistical Yearbook.* Various issues.

Republic of South Africa, Board for the Decentralization of Industry. *Report on the Activities of the Board.* 1 April 1983 to 31 March 1984.

Republic of South Africa, Department of Foreign Affairs. *Manual: The Promotion of Industrial Development as an Element of a Co-ordinated Regional Development Strategy for Southern Africa.* Pretoria: Government Printer, 1982.

Republic of South Africa, Department of Foreign Affairs. *South Africa: Mainstay of Southern Africa.* Pretoria: Government Printer, 1985.

Reynders, H.J.J. "Black Industrial Entrepreneurship." *South African Journal of Economics* 45, no. 3 (September 1977).

Robertson, Hector Menteith. *South Africa: Economic and Political Aspects.* Durham, NC: Duke University Press, 1957.

Rogers, Barbara. *White Wealth and Black Poverty: American Investments in Southern Africa.* Westport, CT: Greenwood Press, 1976.

Sampson, Anthony. *Black and Gold: Tycoons, Revolutionaries and Apartheid.* London: Hodder and Stoughton, 1987.

Savastuk, D.J. "African Tour Reveals Opportunities and Challenges for U.S. Business." *Business in America* 5 (1982).

Schlemmer, Lawrence and Eddie Webster, eds. *Change, Reform and Economic Growth in South Africa.* Johannesburg: Raven Press, 1978.

Schmidt, Elizabeth. *Decoding Corporate Camouflage: U.S. Business Support for Apartheid.* Washington, D.C.: Institute for Policy Studies, 1980.

Schomer, H. "South Africa: Beyond Fair Employment." *Harvard Business Review* 61 (1983).

Schrire, Robert, ed. *South Africa: Public Policy Perspectives.* Cape Town: Juta, 1982.

Schumann, C.G.W. *Structural Change and Business Cycles in South Africa 1806–1936.* London: P.S. King & Son, Ltd., 1938.

Segal, Ronald, ed. *Sanctions Against South Africa.* Harmondsworth: Penguin Books, 1964.

Seidman, Ann and Neva. *South Africa and U.S. Multinational Corporations.* Westport, CT: Lawrence Hill & Co., 1977.

Sherman, S.P. "Scoring Corporate Conflict in South Africa (Sullivan Principles)." *Fortune* 110 (1984).

Simon, W.E. "Our Most Powerful Weapon Against Apartheid (American Corporations Role of Leadership)."*Across the Board* 22 (1985).

Sinclair, Michael. *The Effect of Economic Growth on Social and Political Change in South Africa.* Washington, D.C.: Investor Responsibility Research Center, May 1986.

South African Institute of Race Relations. *Laws Affecting Race Relations in South Africa 1948–1976.* Johannesburg, 1978.

South African Institute of Race Relations. *Survey of Race Relations in South Africa.* Johannesburg, various years.

South African Reserve Bank, *Quarterly Bulletin,* various issues.

South African Reserve Bank, *A Short Historical Review Issued in Commemoration of the Bank's Fiftieth Anniversary, 1921–1971.*

Spandau, Arnt. *Economic Boycott Against South Africa: Normative and Factual Issues.* Cape Town: Juta, 1978.

Spooner, F. *South African Predicament: The Economics of Apartheid.* New York: Praeger, 1961.

Study Commission on U.S. Policy Toward Southern Africa. *South Africa: Time Running Out.* Berkeley: University of California Press, 1981.

"The Sullivan Principles After Six Years: Compliance and Noncompliance." *Business and Society Review* 44 (Winter 1983).

Thompson, Leonard and Andrew Prior. *South African Politics.* New Haven and London: Yale University Press, 1982.

United Nations. "Seminar Calls for Total Embargo on Supply of Oil to

South Africa: Halt Urged to all Types of Nuclear Collaboration." *UN Chronicle* 17 (May 1980).

United Nations, Centre on Transnational Corporations. *Activities of Transnational Corporations in South Africa and Namibia and the Responsibilities of Home Countries with Respect to their Operations in this Area.* New York, 1986.

United Nations, Unit on Apartheid. *Industrialization, Foreign Capital, and Forced Labour in South Africa.* New York, 1970.

UNESCO. *Activities of Transnational Corporations in Southern Africa: Impact on Financial and Social Structures.* Report of the Secretariat. New York, March 16, 1978.

UNIDO, *Industrial Co-operation Through the Southern African Development Coordination Conference.* New York, October 15, 1985.

United States, Department of State. *A U.S. Policy Toward South Africa.* Report on the Secretary of State's Advisory Committee on South Africa. January 1987.

Van Biljon and Frederik Josef. *State Interference in South Africa.* London: P.S. King & Son Ltd., 1939.

Viljoen, S.P. Du T. "Investment in the Private Sector of South Africa." *South African Journal of Economics* 33 (December 1965).

Wheatcroft, Geoffrey. *The Randlords, The Men Who Made South Africa.* London: Widenfeld and Nicolson, 1985.

Wilson, Francis. *Labour in the South African Gold Mines 1911–1969.* London: Cambridge University Press, 1972.

Wilson, Francis. *Migrant Labour in South Africa.* Johannesburg: The South African Council of Churches and SPRO-CAS, 1972.

Wilson, Monica and Leonard Thomson, eds. *The Oxford History of South Africa Vol. II, 1870–1966.* London: Oxford University Press, 1971.

INDEX

ABOUT THE AUTHOR

Stephen R. Lewis, Jr., became President of Carleton College in 1987 after 21 years at Williams College as the Herbert H. Lehman Professor of Economics, Provost, and Chairman of the Economics Department. A specialist in economic policy and planning in developing countries, Lewis was Economic Consultant to the Ministry of Finance and Development Planning of the government of Botswana (1975–1988); Visiting Fellow with the Institute of Development Studies at the University of Sussex (1986–1987); Visiting Senior Research Fellow at the Institute for Development Studies in Kenya (1971–1973); and Economic Advisor to the Ministry of Finance and Economic Planning of the government of Kenya (1971–1974). For his service to the government of Botswana, Lewis was awarded the Presidential Order of Meritous Service in 1983 for "outstanding contributions to Botswana's development." Among the many articles and books of which he is author or co-author are *Taxation for Development* (1984) and *South Africa: Has Time Run Out?* (1986).